HIGHER EDUCATION AND EMPLOYABILITY

HIGHER EDUCATION AND EMPLOYABILITY

*New Models for
Integrating Study and Work*

PETER J. STOKES

Harvard Education Press
Cambridge, Massachusetts

Library of Congress Control Number 2015936475

Paperback ISBN 978-1-61250-826-9
Library Edition ISBN 978-1-61250-827-6

Published by Harvard Education Press,
an imprint of the Harvard Education Publishing Group

Harvard Education Press
8 Story Street
Cambridge, MA 02138

Cover Design: Saizon Design
Cover Image: © newyear/Shutterstock

The typefaces used in this book are Legacy Serif ITC and Knockout

For Paul and Julie,
and all that they discover along the way

CONTENTS

FOREWORD

Peter Stokes's *Higher Education and Employability: New Models for Integrating Study and Work* is a timely and relevant work for anyone interested in the future of human capital development. In the early twenty-first century, economic growth and education scholars have begun to move beyond the concepts of an industrial or knowledge economy toward that of a learning economy—a society in which the capability to learn is critical to the economic success of individuals, firms, regions, and national economies.[1] In a learning economy, the linear relationship between formal higher education and learning in the workplace is becoming obsolete, and this transition is creating pressure for research universities and employers to integrate knowledge creation with job creation and academic teaching with applied learning in order to create sustainable human capital development systems that promote individual competence, business innovation, and global competitiveness. This move requires a deep integration of study and work that redefines the relationship between colleges and universities and employers and new forms of partnership to encompass it. Through the lens of employability, Stokes outlines this new ecosystem of learning partnerships that embrace the learning economy paradigm and provides a guide to emergent best practice and organizational transformation for both employers and higher education institutions.

EDUCATION AND HUMAN CAPITAL DEVELOPMENT

In their landmark 2010 book *The Race Between Education and Technology,* economists Lawrence F. Katz and Claudia Goldin document the rise of the United States as an economic powerhouse and the catalytic role education played in the process.[2] Through econometric modeling, the authors demonstrate that for any given decade in the twentieth century the increasing education attainment of successive age cohorts accounted for 25–30 percent of GDP growth. They conclude that if the twentieth century was "the American Century," then this exceptionalism was almost certainly driven by human capital development.

Katz and Goldin view human capital development largely through the lens of the emergence and evolution of public schooling, the key highlights of which include the common school (elementary and middle school) movement (1840–1860), the high school movement (1910–1940), and the shift to mass college education (1950–). They contend that from the mid-nineteenth century to today, the United States has led the world in creating the platforms for successive levels of human capital development: "By the early 20th Century America educated its youth to a far greater extent than did most, if not every, European country. Secondary schools in America were free and generally accessible, whereas they were costly and often inaccessible in Europe. Even in the 1930s America was virtually alone in providing universally free and accessible public schools. The United States expanded its lead in education in the 20th Century by instituting mass secondary schooling and then establishing a flexible and multifaceted higher education system."[3]

Goldin and Katz characterize the beginnings of these movements as highly varied, grassroots efforts based on several pillars: public funding, public provision, local decentralization, separation of church and state, gender neutrality, and open and forgiving access. In other words, while we take our (public) K–12 and higher education systems for granted, they emerged from an ecosystem of local interests and trial and error to become a more or less interconnected, effective system that helps the nation develop human capital—citizens, entrepreneurs, workers, public leaders, parents. And as we move deeper into the twenty-first century, we need to educate ever more citizens to postsecondary levels as a means to prepare them for economic opportunity and competitiveness in the learning economy.

Higher Education and Employability is a significant addition to the growing body of literature on the practical realities of educating individuals for success in the global learning and innovation economy, specifically focusing on the role of research universities. Stokes's use of the concept of employability as a bridge between higher education as an academic enterprise and employers facilitated by the emergence of an ecosystem of organizations that help integrate formal learning into practical life and work is valuable on two fronts. First, the employability concept helps mend the artificial divide between vocational and academic learning that evolved with the industrial economy. Second, by unbundling needs and services embedded in the employability concept, Stokes frames an ecosystem for integrating work and learning to help us better understand how component pieces may evolve into new partnerships and business models. So as Goldin and Katz helped us understand the chaotic evolution of public education in the United States,

Stokes helps us understand the importance of integrating study and work.

EMPLOYABILITY—A BRIDGE BETWEEN ACADEMIC AND VOCATIONAL LEARNING

Employability means different things to different people. In the case of the dialogue between higher education institutions and employers about necessary knowledge and skills, these different meanings often devolve into hardened positions on education versus training or on people as human beings not just workers. Thus, Stokes wisely avoids creating a hard-and-fast definition. Rather, by unpacking the ecosystem of tools and services emerging at the intersection of universities and employers, he turns employability into a conceptual bridge that integrates academic and vocational/applied learning within a twenty-first-century understanding of human capital development. This is most useful, because being free of industrial-era notions of human capital development is a key step in allowing for new practices, tools, and partnerships to emerge and in helping the nation reclaim its lead in human capital development.

Stokes's research university case studies—Georgia Institute of Technology, New York University (NYU), and Northeastern University—each model this freedom. They purposefully exist at the nexus between academic and professional knowledge and skills development and the flow of talent into the global workforce. Stokes's description of NYU's vision for itself reflects this thinking: it is first and foremost an urban institution and increasingly a global institution that is bringing a compelling value proposition to a set of world markets by combining a deep commitment to the liberal arts and academic research with a pragmatic and long-standing focus on professional education. These institutions stand out as exemplars of the employability ecosystem that integrates study and work through employer and university partnerships. Yet, to fully understand their importance to the evolution of higher education, we must delve deeper to the roots of the academic–vocational education divide.

The emergence of the industrial, mass production economy forms the broader context from which the early education movements sprang. Paradoxically, while the industrial economy made clear the need to provide broad-based education, it also introduced a growing distinction between academic and vocational learning. In the first half of the twentieth century, as automation and assembly lines increasingly drove production and competitive advantage, workers came to be perceived as needing only the skills necessary to follow rules and the machine systems. Leaders, in contrast, needed higher-order thinking skills to manage companies growing in size and complexity.[4] This type of thinking was enshrined in Frederick Taylor's 1911 book *Principles of Scientific Management,* which emphasized breaking down production tasks to simplest rules so workers could follow them. As a result of this black-and-white demarcation of knowledge and skills, the idea of combining higher education, exemplified by the liberal arts, and training, demonstrated by vocational-professional curricula, became a nonstarter.

Further into the century human resource scholars moved beyond the simple workers "do" and leaders "think" framework to recognize a deeper architecture of knowledge in organizations that envisioned a portfolio of four knowledge areas and skills needed for an organization to thrive: general, job/occupation specific, firm/agency specific, and industry specific.[5] This new framework provided a tool for unpacking the evolution of roles in the higher education system. In light of the worker/leader dichotomy, educational institutions grew up to provide different types of learning to these two distinct groups. Four-year colleges and universities provided general knowledge and high-level professional (industry) knowledge to managers. Community colleges, technical schools, and employers provided firm- and job-specific knowledge to workers. Thus, a myth that academic and vocational education must always be separate was embedded into higher education delivery systems. As important, employers' connections to higher education, to the extent they existed, were relegated to training-oriented programs.

In the twenty-first century, however, the competitive imperative to innovate products, services, and even business models has caused a democratization of the organizational knowledge and skills portfolio. For firms, the four knowledge areas are becoming more blurred, with frontline workers requiring more of the education traditionally reserved for managers and managers needing the frontline knowledge that allows for rapid prototyping in response to changing demand. For individual workers, managers, and entrepreneurs, the competitive imperative drives a need to be continuously building knowledge, skills, abilities, and networks in an increasingly dynamic labor market with many career changes and company start-ups. Further, the democratization of organizational knowledge and the acceleration of competition has been shortening the time window for human capital development. Employers are increasingly seeking individuals with both technical knowledge in their field and practical experience solving workplace problems. Of course, employers have always valued experience in more seasoned veterans; what is changing is the emphasis on applied problem-solving skills in newer workers. According to global competitiveness expert and Harvard Business School professor Michael Porter, "Competitive workers must have the ability to apply academic or technical knowledge to solve real-world problems . . . and to work effectively with other people as customers, coworkers and supervisors."[6]

The research university employability ecosystem that Stokes lays out covers a broad landscape, from co-ops to academic courses, to career coaching, to job matching, to peer networks, to internships, and more. Georgia Tech's Design Expo uses actual industry challenges to create applied learning experiences for students in collaboration with industry partners. NYU leverages three global campuses and alumni to create internship and service opportunities with multinational corporations and foreign governments. Northeastern University offers the ALIGN program (Accelerated Link to Industry through Northeastern's Global Network) to provide a bridge to careers for new graduates or career changers through a hybrid of online courses and experiential learning opportunities.

In Stokes's employability ecosystem, the more university-centric models are mirrored by a rich diversity of organizations essentially unbundling employability services and adding value back into employers and universities by facilitating the integration of study and work. In recruiting and matching services for students and employers, there are start-ups like Gild, Pymetrics, and Kalibrr. The entrepreneurial venture Koru provides a bridge to employment by upgrading the business skills of liberal arts graduates. Collegefeed, Evisors, and Doostang provide job-matching opportunities for graduates. And Degreed and Accredible are developing new ways of validating what people know and can do for both employers and universities.

Each of these unbundled employability solutions is delivered in various blended forms—hi-touch/hi-tech, college outsourced service, employer insourced service, intermediary organizations. This is a diverse set of solutions, yet they are all encompassed by the employability concept that catalyzes academic learning with experiential learning, mentoring, recruiting, job matching, and credentialing in a broad human capital development ecosystem which acknowledges that knowledge development and deployment in a learning economy are not linear but dynamic and recursive. Stokes notes the sentiment of one University of Pennsylvania interviewee who could "envision a future where students may spend close to a year on campus to experience the benefits of building a network and then enter the workforce and enroll on a subscription basis to have access to a library of just-in-time education resources in the form of an online 'mini-course,' meaning that the model shifts from one of 'learn-learn-learn-certify-wait-wait-wait-deploy' to one of 'learn-certify-deploy, learn-certify-deploy.'"

Stokes's consistent and compelling theme, captured by the employability concept, is that twenty-first-century human capital development isn't an either/or proposition; rather, it is both an academic and an applied learning process requiring many, and new, higher education institution and employer partnerships. The myth of academic versus vocational learning embedded in higher education delivery systems begins to unravel, leading to the natural question—What's next?

FROM ECOSYSTEM TO VALUE CHAIN/MARKETPLACE

The second contribution Stokes brings to the literature is his detailed, and almost real-time, illustration of the unbundling of services that surround the transition from higher education to employment. The set of employability activities and actors he describes, from Degreed to General Assembly to Koru to Northeastern University, covers such a breadth of emergent and innovative practices in human capital development that one cannot discern a mature business model, value chain, or marketplace. Stokes posits an emergent value chain that calls for thoughtful study with regard to sustainability.

Stokes's detailed ecosystem description offers clues about how the marketplace may mature and sustain viable partnerships.[7] To explore the potential market impact of these clues, we can use concepts from the innovation literature. Among these key concepts are understanding the distinction between sustaining innovation and disruptive innovation, using enabling technologies, employing business model analysis, and forming value chains and standards. Sustaining innovation is when technology is applied in a way that makes it easier to deploy people and processes to better serve existing customers. In contrast, disruptive innovation is when technology is applied in a way that creates a simpler, more affordable product for a new group of customers who, in most cases, were not buying (or succeeding in) the traditional offering.

Stokes's ecosystem contains both types of innovations. Boot camp experiences from Koru to General Assembly currently serve the best customers of higher education—students who attend relatively selective institutions—so in many ways they can be seen as sustaining and adding to the existing offering. Similarly, Northeastern's co-op model going global is most arguably a sustaining innovation. Yet organizations such as Degreed and LinkedIn are positing entirely different ways of recognizing competence and credentialing it, a service historically reserved for colleges and universities. If they succeed, employability recognitions will be introduced to many more actors in the market. Even research universities are moving toward disruption. For example, Georgia Tech's partnership with AT&T on the use of massive open online courses (MOOCs) to create an innovative online master's degree program in computer science for $8,000 could end up being a truly disruptive innovation.

Many of the employability ecosystem actors and organizations depend on Web-enabled platforms that make learning tools and labor/education market intelligence more readily available and communicable. Technology enablers as a requisite for innovation are thus highly visible in the market. Given that employability is about the integration of academic and applied learning opportunities, the driver of market growth and value-added partnership will be those technologies that enable deep integration. Northeastern University's virtual co-op approach (the ALIGN program) is one to watch in this regard. It has the potential to demonstrate the ability to scale the use of technology in experiential learning in heretofore unheard of ways.

A simple enough business model typology encompasses three basic types: a solution shop, which tackles hard-to-define (and -solve) market challenges; a value-added process shop (VAP), which organizes inputs through defined processes to create offerings of higher value; and facilitated user networks, which enable participants to exchange value with each other. A defining characteristic for each business model is how payment is made. Solution shops that receive a fee for services rendered are less tied to outcomes because they are tougher to predict. VAPs develop methodical ways of organizing resources to achieve certain outcomes with regularity and are paid for achieving the outcome. And facilitated user networks are paid for by a subscription to or membership in the platform.

Stokes's employability ecosystem encompasses all these models. A relevant question is whether any given entrant has identified the correct business model. For instance, Hack Reactor, a twelve-week program that bills itself as an equivalent to a traditional computer science degree with job placement and charges $18,000, is positioning itself as a VAP with guaranteed outcomes. It may be too early to know if it can deliver the equivalent of a computer science degree given its time and cost parameters. This sets up the potential for failure within the market. With regard to the research universities, a key will be what type of business model is a given innovation. The NY You Knowledge Commons is an interesting example. It is a technology-enabled, closed mentoring network limited to NYU alumni and community members. It is a facilitated user network business model. Hence, it should be funded by a membership fee. How does this model fit with the pricing for the core education offering that could be considered a VAP? When does someone begin to move into the NY You?

The final two components, value chain formation and standards, are highly interrelated.

With business models still forming, it is difficult to see how to extend employability value chains that might link different, distinct services (e.g., mentor connections, experiential learning, labor market matching) in a sustainable, coherent way. Right now the ecosystem is experimenting with organization and partner boundaries and value propositions.

One key to how these early experiments may play out is the evolution of standards that will guide quality and interoperability of business across the employability ecosystem. For example, in the competency-based learning space, the Degree Qualifications Profile (DQP) initiative, supported by the Lumina Foundation for Education, is a framework for illustrating what students should be expected to know and be able to do once they earn their postsecondary degrees. The initiative proposes specific learning outcomes and competencies that benchmark the certificates and associate, bachelor's, and master's degrees along five dimensions: applied learning, intellectual skills, specialized knowledge, broad knowledge, and civic learning. Employability ecosystem players could leverage the DQP standard to seamlessly rebundle a set of services from competency-based classroom learning to workplace-based learning projects to employer match. The DQP would provide the lingua franca that allows disparate players to deliver quality and responsive services, thus forming a sustainable value network. There are similar standards that could be brought to bear in career coaching, peer-to-peer networks, etc. Robust standards will likely form the foundation of the best value chains, so actors in the employability space should seek out these activities for partnership first. For example, could Koru, Degreed, and Georgia Tech, through its $8,000 master's degree, create a new value chain for preparing and credentialing skilled computer science professionals on demand based on the DQP backbone? Or could Northeastern combine its ALIGN program with Accredible and GILD to create a value chain for preparing career changers in faster and more affordable ways?

As Stokes's ecosystem methodically evolves toward maturity, we should continue to observe and invest in the innovations that bear up under these analytical tools. Further, as higher education institutions and employers develop the competence to manage both sustaining and disruptive innovations in the employability ecosystem, it will be exciting to watch the new human capital development system emerge. I suspect that both higher education institutions and employers will look quite different when it does. As Stokes writes, "We may well need to go beyond thinking about how education prepares students for work and begin thinking about how education reaches, informs, and develops a different kind of character: the *student-employee,* who is both a learner and a current or future worker." This reimagining posits learning economy thinking that will shape the structures and futures of employers and higher education institutions alike.

In today's learning economy, the integration of study and work at research universities will be key to America winning the next leg of the race between education and technology. Indeed, Peter Stokes has provided a useful guide for understanding how the integration of study and work at research universities will form a human capital development system for the twenty-first century.

—Louis Soares
Vice President of Policy Research and Strategy,
American Council on Education

MAKING A DIFFERENCE

What should colleges and universities be doing differently to assist their students in preparing for the world of work? That's the question that *Higher Education and Employability* sets out to answer.

It may be worth pausing right here, however, before venturing any further.

If some readers already feel a bit uncomfortable with the implied proposition that colleges and universities should be doing anything differently at all, that's not altogether surprising. Moreover, they may wonder why I assume that institutions of higher learning should be burdened with a responsibility for workforce development when historically that obligation has mostly fallen elsewhere, and that's not an entirely unfair question either. Also, they may certainly feel that there are other more pressing issues facing higher education today—the sustainability of public funding models, increased regulation, activist trustees, the future of the humanities, rising tuition, student debt, and the growing anxiety about whether or not a college degree is worth the cost anymore, among numerous other matters of admittedly real importance.

I can appreciate those concerns. Many within the higher education community feel under almost constant attack, and seemingly from all sides. From legislators with tight purse strings, from reform-minded administrators and boards, from Silicon Valley entrepreneurs seeking to reinvent education as we know it, from parents, policy makers, and the press and many others besides, including the authors of books about higher education, many, if not all, of whom seem to want colleges and universities to do something (at times seemingly almost anything) differently.

This book is not an attack on higher education. To the contrary, in these pages I advocate for a particular mode of education that is already woven into the fabric of some of our best institutions, one that couples academic rigor with professional preparation in sensible ways, and this advocacy extends to my promoting the notion that this mode of education should be more common than it is today and should take root across a greater variety of institutions. Of course, institutions of higher education can only achieve so much. They cannot by themselves change their local economic environment or create jobs out of thin air. I do not argue that they should be able to do so. And a college education alone cannot, of course, be expected to prepare an individual for the world of work in all the many ways that she will ultimately need to be prepared. But colleges and universities can strengthen the relevance of their academic and cocurricular programs in ways that improve the job prospects of their graduates, and they will be in a much better position to achieve that if they demonstrate a willingness to work more closely with employers that seek new talent, and, in turn, if those employers reciprocate that willingness to partner with institutions in deeper ways.

Furthermore, there is good reason for education providers and employers to attempt such collaborations: students need jobs, and the health of the economy depends, in no small measure, on their getting them.

Sociologists Richard Arum and Josipa Roksa, whose 2011 book *Academically Adrift* faulted American colleges and universities for not doing enough to challenge students in the context of their academic studies, released a follow-on analysis in 2014, *Aspiring Adults Adrift*, in which they examine the early career experiences of a number of the students whose data was the focus of their initial study. The new book paints a picture of widespread underemployment. In response, Arum calls for more extensive development of institutional programs "that facilitate school-to-work transitions, in terms of internships, apprenticeships, job placement programs."[1] Invited to weigh in on the thesis of Arum and Roksa's latest work, Anthony P. Carnevale, director of the Georgetown University Center on Education and the Workforce, commented that although higher education in the United States "really is a work-force-development system," higher education "doesn't like to see itself that way."[2]

Writing in a 2014 *Salon* commentary timed to coincide with the back-to-school season, former secretary of labor and currently Chancellor's Professor of Public Policy at the Goldman School of Public Policy at the University of California, Berkeley, Robert Reich took aim at another target: American businesses, which he faulted for not being sufficiently involved in curriculum design, particularly in the realm of technical education. In contrast to America, Reich wrote about how "Germany provides its students the alternative of a world-class technical education that's kept the German economy at the forefront of precision manufacturing and applied technology. The skills taught are based on industry standards, and courses are designed by businesses that need the graduates. So when young Germans get their degrees, jobs are waiting for them."[3]

Throughout these pages I argue that employers and institutions must consider how better to redefine a shared interest in promoting employability and work readiness among today's students and recent graduates and then work to achieve it through real collaboration. Both sides must come to the table—our colleges and universities, as Arum, Roksa, and Carnevale argue, and our employers, as Reich argues. In this book I take the position that the responsibility to educate individuals while preparing them for the world of work is a shared responsibility of education providers and employers. Both sides have much to gain from such collaboration, and both sides have been too slow to develop the deeper collaborations required to effectively couple education and preparation for the world of work. If it can be said that anyone is at fault for not achieving such collaborations already, then such blame cannot be laid at the doorsteps of colleges and universities alone. Employers, too, must become more activated, engaged, and prepared to help.

The argument I put forward, then, is not in any way anti-institution, anti-faculty, anti–liberal arts, or anti-education-for-education's-sake. I view the combination of academic study and work preparation as a *both/and* rather than an *either/or* proposition. For these reasons, this book does not take the form of a critical appraisal of contemporary curricula; nor does it offer a critique of the return on investment for the average student pursuing an average degree at an average institution. To some readers, though, it may look like some or all of those things.

To those readers, I apologize in advance. Unfortunately, in these often polarizing times, that kind of perceived contentiousness occasionally comes with the territory. But it's not my intention to foment any ill will among the great numbers of good people working on the front lines of higher education day in and day out or to underestimate the value of the work they contribute even as I explore the potential for their institutions to offer more.

I do, in fact, feel comfortable asserting that colleges and universities can and should do more to assist their students in preparing for the world of work, and in this book I attempt to offer one possible answer to the question, *What should institutions be doing differently?*

I do so by examining the diverse ways that college and universities, employers, education startups, and other organizations are attempting to integrate study and work in new ways in order to forge a more seamless path for students as they make the journey from education to employment. I set out to do this both with an eye toward identifying a number of extant, practical models for engaging in this kind of work as well as in order to imagine the opportunities that remain for education providers and employers to achieve a still more intentional, aligned, and effective integration of study and work to support the employability and work readiness of our current and future graduates—all with the aim of helping students to find a path to good jobs and to support the growth of our economy.

More particularly, I aim to illustrate, through a small number of focused case studies, how closer strategic collaboration among institutions that produce graduates and organizations that hire them can improve educational and professional outcomes for all stakeholders. To that end, I intend for this book to help inform higher education leaders, corporate executives, and policy makers about how these goals have been and can be achieved, as well as to suggest how objectives such as these can be realized at greater scale going forward. These cases can serve as models for other institutions and employers to replicate in their own fashion and can also inform policy leaders as they consider how best to advance relevant, high-impact policy initiatives that promote the work readiness and employability of greater numbers of students.

While there is a substantial body of work examining the role of community colleges, government agencies, professional associations, and other diverse organizations collaborating with industry to support workforce development (including projects such as the BioNetwork in North Carolina, Project Quest in Texas, or the Automotive Manufacturing Training and Education Collective [AMTEC] that works across a dozen U.S. states), there is a need for significant studies examining the role of research universities engaging in such collaborations.[4]

Why focus on research universities? Totaling fewer than three hundred institutions and enrolling approximately a quarter of all postsecondary students, research universities may not touch the largest number of learners, but they do serve a particular segment of students who seek to engage in particular kinds of work and at particular professional levels in some of the most rapidly evolving industries and at some of the world's most innovative employers, including large companies and startups, government agencies, and nonprofit organizations.[5] Furthermore, research universities bring particular assets to bear in their efforts to develop talent, support research and development, and promote knowledge creation on regional, national, and, increasingly, global levels. For those reasons, the role of research universities in stimulating talent development through the integration of study and work is worthy of reflection and analysis alongside the other sorts of institutions and organizations that are more frequently associated with matters of workforce development.

In the past, it might have seemed safe to assume, however rightly or wrongly, that for a certain type of institution, the employability of its graduates would be achieved without special effort. Today, however, it would be risky to take too much for granted about the work readiness of students from all sorts of institutions. And if matters such as workforce development (a phrase that for many connotes vocational training) have historically been issues for community colleges, for-profit institutions, and other sorts of organizations to address, in the present moment the responsibility to address the challenges associated with employability and work readiness must fall to all types of institutions and all types of employers.

Thus, while I set out to provide an overview of the diversity of institutions and organizations currently innovating in the area of employability, at its heart, this study focuses on three case analyses of collaborations between research universities and employers to illustrate the particular kinds of contributions these sorts of institutions can make relative to talent development. The case studies of the Georgia Institute of Technology, New York University (NYU), and Northeastern University highlight collaborations with employers to design more market-relevant curricula, to foster more meaningful experiential learning opportunities, and to connect students with industry mentors who can provide relevant professional coaching, among other initiatives—all in support of fostering work readiness and employability through the integration of study and work.

Of course, by no means do these few cases represent a comprehensive review of university-employer collaborations to foster work readiness, nor should these institutions necessarily be regarded as the foremost exemplars of this kind of endeavor. These sorts of collaborations are too nascent and too rapidly evolving for any institution to stake a claim at being a genuine exemplar. Furthermore, there are too many aspects to the effort of integrating study and work for any single institution to rise to the level of representing a comprehensive, mature, or singular model. The cases highlighted here are by no means the only ones that could have been studied, but they have been selected for a number reasons: their representativeness (a mix of public and private, of technically focused and liberal arts programs, of undergraduate-level and graduate-level offerings, of online and place-based delivery models), their interest in serving multiple geographic markets, and, most importantly, their concerted efforts to enhance their graduates' work readiness by thinking differently about how best to support the development of talent at scale in partnership with local, national, international, and multinational employers.

What these case analyses help illustrate is that making a difference in better preparing college graduates for the world of work requires institutions and their employer partners to think differently about the integration of study and work.

1

DROWNPROOFING 2.0

In 1940, a swimming instructor at the Georgia Institute of Technology by the name of Fred Lanoue—known affectionately to his students as Crankshaft due to a limp he had acquired while in the Navy—introduced a daunting new course into the university curriculum called Drownproofing, during which students were thrown into a pool with their hands and feet bound. Crankshaft's job was to teach these students how to maintain a vertical floating position and effectively manage their breathing in order to survive in the water for long periods under challenging circumstances.

In time, the twenty-two-hour water survival course became a graduation requirement at Georgia Tech, striking fear into the hearts of swimmers and nonswimmers alike, many of whom put off taking Drowning 101, as it became known, until their senior year. As well as inspiring fear among students, though, the course also signaled the resolve and toughness of Georgia Tech's graduates, and it became a revered tradition on campus well into the late 1980s, when it ceased to be a required course.[1]

The spirit of drownproofing lives on at Georgia Tech, however, as Steve McLaughlin, the chair of the School of Electrical and Computer Engineering, explained to me in the winter of 2014. Think of it as Drownproofing 2.0, McLaughlin said: "Tying students' hands and feet together and throwing them in the pool—that ended more than twenty years ago. But a 'drownproofing' life skill is something we still do today. It's survival under pressure. It gives you a confidence that you can't get any other way. And today the life skill that everyone has to have is the ability to create their own job. That's Drownproofing 2.0."[2]

THE ROLE OF HIGHER EDUCATION IN PROMOTING WORK READINESS

Undoubtedly, there are many within the higher education community who, even today, would reject the notion that the purpose of a college education is to prepare students for the world of work, much less to train students to become job creators themselves. Yet, for others, the task of fostering students' work readiness, developing their entrepreneurial capabilities, and guiding them down a pathway to a successful career is the de facto mission of all of our colleges and universities.

For the former group, the growing focus on jobs is inevitably viewed as reductivist, relegating higher education institutions to the same status as factories churning out "product"—skilled labor, in this case. "Just wait," this constituency might well caution, "this vocational turn will be accompanied by a hail of unintended consequences: a weakened citizenry, the abandonment of the arts, and the valorization of rote learning in place of critical thinking."

For the latter group, the increased attention to graduates' employability and work readiness signals a long-overdue shift to a more realistic perspective on the function of higher education within a knowledge economy. "Look," this group of stakeholders might well argue, "preparing future professionals to master basic problem-solving skills, arrive at work on time, communicate effectively, escalate challenges to managers only when warranted, and possess some familiarity with the tools of the contemporary workplace (whether spreadsheets, algorithms, databases, etc.) just makes good, practical sense."

Both sides have a point, even if neither side necessarily sees the whole of the matter. But the contemporary moment, characterized as it is by rapidly evolving industries and global economic uncertainty, may require all of us within the higher education community to think in terms of both/and rather than either/or propositions about the purpose of a college education. Certainly, the proponents of employability—who are by no means necessarily antagonistic toward civic virtue, the arts, or critical thinking—appear to be in the ascendency just now, spurred on by an extended economic crisis as well as by the concern that too many recent graduates are unemployed or underemployed. Some institutions, for example, are now going so far as to offer employment guarantees to their graduates, as is the case at Davenport University in Michigan.[3] Indeed, there is accumulating evidence that a perspective committed to fostering employability is taking greater hold both within the higher education community itself and more broadly in the realm of public opinion and even public policy.

In the summer of 2013, for example, President Obama proposed a new federal rating system for colleges and universities that would focus on, among other things, graduates' earnings.[4] Despite considerable pushback from many within the higher education community, President Obama continued to argue on behalf of the merits of his proposed "scorecard" for colleges and universities in the months that followed, even while acknowledging his critics: "A lot of colleges and universities say, you know, if you start ranking just based on cost and employability, et cetera, you're missing the essence of higher education."[5] But the president also argued that his scorecard is modest in its ambitions and practical in its areas of focus: "So you have just a general sense of what's the typical graduation rate, what's the typical debt that you carry once you get out, what is the employment rate for graduates five years afterwards."

By the summer of 2014, the Obama administration outlined further courses of action, announcing a series of initiatives focused explicitly on job training and employability, allocating $1.4 billion in grants to be made available to institutions that follow a "job-driven checklist" designed to promote employer engagement, apprenticeships and internships, data-driven accountability, regional economic development partnerships, and "a seamless progression from one educational stepping stone to another," among other actions.[6] It identified three principal benefits it expected to result from its efforts to support industry and educator collaboration: "getting long-term unemployed Americans back to work," "upskilling American workers through apprenticeships and on-the-job training," and providing "accelerated training for in-demand information technology jobs across the economy."

The effort to promote apprenticeships and other experiences that better prepare individuals for the workforce is laudable, and undoubtedly necessary, as the United States has relatively few apprenticeships compared to other nations. A recent report from the Hamilton Project noted that apprentices "make up only 0.2 percent of the U.S. labor force, far less than in Canada (2.2 percent), Britain (2.7 percent), and Australia and Germany (3.7 percent)."[7]

At the same time as the president promotes his initiatives, governors and other state leaders have hardly been sitting idly by waiting for the federal government to sort out these challenges. Ohio, for example, is investing $12 million on its OhioMeansJobs.com Web site to assist students in better understanding which college majors are likely to lead to jobs in high-growth industries.[8] Numerous other states are also attempting to create greater transparency regarding the employment statistics of graduates who have attended their colleges and universities, in some cases aided by third-party organizations such as CollegeMeasures, which works with states as diverse as Florida, Texas, Virginia, and Arkansas, among others.[9]

Journalists have not been shy about picking up on this theme either, particularly in the business press. Publications such as the *Wall Street Journal, Forbes*, and the *Financial Times* have published numerous stories in recent years about college graduates purportedly lacking the skills employers require. Occasionally these articles highlight the need for closer collaboration among employers and colleges to address the so-called skills gap, whether through apprenticeships or by allowing employers a greater role in designing curriculum or through other means.

Rankings organizations are also bringing greater attention to the matter of work readiness. The QS World University Rankings released in the late summer of 2014 were widely reported by the media as assessing global institutions on their achievements with respect to teaching, research, and employability, with QS placing the Massachusetts Institute of Technology (MIT) at the top of its current ranking.[10]

Think tanks, consultancies, and research firms have weighed in as well. In a report published in early 2014 by the consulting firm FSG, released to coincide with the World Economic Forum in Davos, Switzerland, Harvard Business School guru Michael Porter argued that "no longer are companies content to wait at the end of the education pipeline for graduates with the right skills. Instead they are becoming part of the pipeline itself, taking on themselves many of the roles historically reserved for education institutions."[11] Consider, for example, the case of Northrop Grumman Corp., which recently partnered with the University of Maryland to design a new curriculum in cyber security. Northrop Grumman not only helped fund the development of the curriculum, but it also provided computers as well as funding toward the cost of building a new dorm to house the program's students.[12]

Nor have higher education leaders failed to take a position on these issues. In early 2014, Nancy Zimpher, the chancellor of the State University of New York system, announced a bold expansion of the SUNY Works program with the stated aim of creating partnerships with all Fortune 500 companies operating throughout the state to support cooperative education initiatives, internships, service learning, community service, and other practical learning experiences.[13] And writing in a *Chronicle of Higher Education* commentary just days after Zimpher's announcement, Drexel University president John Fry argued that our colleges and universities "won't be able to create more-tangible returns on investment for our graduates unless the rapidly expanding chasm between what higher education institutions produce and what employers want is closed. Access to a college education is no longer enough. The world has changed so significantly that colleges and universities must complement traditional education with real experience, including authentic connections to the workplace."[14]

Clearly, there is much pressure for colleges and universities to do more to prepare their students for the world of work. Georgia Tech's McLaughlin may be right. Today, the ability to land a job is a critical life skill. And the role of the college or university in fostering this ability among its students is relevant not just to those individual students but to whole economic regions, to nations, and, inevitably, to the world at large. Certainly the global economic crisis of the last half-dozen years has concentrated our collective attention, both here in the United States and around the world, on the need for jobs and the need for strategies to support meaningful economic growth. As McLaughlin's comments imply, postsecondary institutions have an important role to play in stimulating economic growth, and in no small measure they can accomplish this by developing the capacities within their students to not only achieve strong academic outcomes but to succeed in the world of work and even to thrive as entrepreneurs.

Of course, colleges and universities cannot shoulder that burden alone. If they are to successfully prepare students for the world of work, they must be capable of equipping them to succeed in a particular context, in certain labor markets requiring specific skills. Consequently, understanding the needs of those labor markets requires colleges and universities to be in dialogue with employers on a continuous basis. Fry, from Drexel, understands that the responsibility for cooperation around education and employment is, as a consequence, necessarily a shared one: "Employers must understand that if they feel the business environment has become too competitive for them to provide training and apprenticeship programs, then expectations of graduates' being work-force-ready are unrealistic. Unless, that is, they commit to work with colleges in creating innovative programs that will help graduates hit the workplace floor running."[15]

Certainly there remain many within the higher education community who would continue to promote education for education's sake and reject the perceived vocationalization of learning in service to the changing whims of employers. But, at the same time, a growing number of higher education institutions clearly view framing the choices faced by colleges and universities in this way as a false dichotomy, and these institutions are demonstrating an increasingly urgent readiness to embrace what we might think of as the Drownproofing 2.0 imperative.

In a June 2014 interview, for example, David Angel, president of Clark University, observed, "I think most colleges and universities would say that their students are well educated at the point of graduation. Question is, do they have the skills that are needed to take that education and add value to the organization that they going to join after graduation?"[16] He went on to say, "I think we've reached the point where there's a growing consensus that what we're looking for, if you like, is liberal education 2.0," a new type of education combining "the critical thinking, good writing, [and] rigor of analysis in the major" associated with the liberal arts with opportunities to place students in "authentic problem-solving situations" where they can demonstrate "resilience." Not only is this the right thing to do for students, their parents, and employers, Angel argued, it's also the right thing to do for the institutions. "Our applications for undergraduate enrollment at Clark are up 70 percent over the last two years."

Angel is not alone in thinking this way about liberal education. Following a survey it conducted in 2013, the labor market data company Burning Glass concluded that the employability of liberal arts students can be enhanced if they can acquire certain complementary skills in areas related to social media, computer programming, sales, graphic design, data analysis, and more. "Despite the high unemployment rate for liberal arts graduates, we are seeing that the skills they possess are in-demand when coupled with specific technical skills," reported

Burning Glass CEO Matthew Sigelman. "Employers report a strong need for recent graduates who possess skills such as writing, adaptability, and problem solving. When combining these skills with workforce-specific competencies, a liberal arts education becomes highly valuable."[17]

PRODUCING THE "GRADUATE PLUS"

While higher education institutions and employers have long worked side by side to better prepare and develop skilled workers and to strengthen the capabilities of management and leadership, and thereby support a strong economy, the need for closer collaboration and tighter alignment between these sectors has arguably never been more critical.

Historically, it's fair to say, the collaboration between higher education institutions and employers has been at arm's length—close but not touching. There are, of course, many examples, both historical and current, of sponsored research collaborations, workforce development initiatives, philanthropic projects, and more. But the kind of collaboration SUNY's Zimpher, Drexel's Fry, and Clark's Angel have called for are of a different sort, focusing on work readiness, curriculum design, internships, problem-based learning, apprenticeships, and other forms of experiential learning, both at the undergraduate and graduate level. These represent newer, emerging forms of university-employer partnerships intended to operate at scale. They bring with them many challenges, and they surface many conflicts, with the values of one sort of educator pitted against those of another sort of educator, or with the values of employers pitted against those of colleges and universities.

Of course, historically, the general absence of deep collaboration between degree-granting institutions and employers in areas such as curriculum design, cocurricular experiences, and education delivery models has produced problems of its own, not the least of which is the sometimes redundant and inefficient societal investments in higher education and corporate training. The absence of deep collaboration has also almost certainly contributed to the growing perception that labor markets are struggling to overcome a serious skills gap, where open jobs go unfilled due to a perceived inadequate supply of skilled labor, and where unemployed or underemployed individuals possessing college degrees fail to realize their full potential.

Those institutions and employer organizations that are exploring deeper forms of collaboration in these areas have the potential to demonstrate something new: namely, how a shared effort at defining the focus, purpose, and relevance of an educational program can achieve a more effective integration of study and work—such as through the design of curriculum informed by industry, the promotion of problem-based learning, and the proliferation of experiential learning opportunities such as internships, apprenticeships, and co-ops—that reaches many rather than only a few and that ultimately rewards individuals, improves talent pools, and drives economic growth.

"A degree, once considered the passport to a graduate-level career, needs to now come in a total package—'graduate plus'—as employers seek well-rounded employees who are 'work-ready' with clear evidence of both job-specific skills and prized graduate attributes," writes Wendy Purcell, president of Plymouth University in the United Kingdom. "Given the fact that more people are achieving graduate status, we need to help our students develop employability attributes and skills throughout their time at university while they study.

This needs careful curriculum and indeed pedagogic innovation and stewardship, including partnerships with business, industry and the professions."[18]

WORK READINESS AS A SHARED RESPONSIBILITY

Late in 2012, Mona Mourshed and her colleagues at the McKinsey Center for Government released a first report in their Education to Employment series that brought the need for this type of collaboration into sharp focus. That initial study, "Education to Employment: Designing a System That Works," looks at global youth unemployment challenges and the roles of higher education institutions and employers in helping students more successfully make the transition from one domain to the other. A second report, "Education to Employment: Getting Europe's Youth into Work," released in January 2014, takes a geographically more narrow look at the same issues and makes some practical recommendations with respect to addressing the apparent gap between recent graduates' capabilities and the skills demanded by employers. Taken together, the reports underscore the potential long-term risks of youth unemployment and underemployment, as well as the challenges facing colleges and universities in cultivating work readiness among their graduates.

One of the problems with attempting to foster work readiness is the difficulty of getting diverse constituencies to agree on what readiness looks like. The results of a survey undertaken in Europe by McKinsey are telling: "74 percent of education providers were confident that their graduates were prepared for work, yet only 38 percent of youth and 35 percent of employers agreed."[19] It will be difficult for postsecondary institutions and employers to collaborate in deeper and more effective ways if their expectations regarding readiness are so divergent.

In response to this difficulty, McKinsey offers some sensible advice: "To improve student prospects, education providers could work more closely with employers to make sure that they are offering courses that really help young people prepare for the workplace."[20] Of course, however sensible advice such as this may appear to be, its simplicity will not necessarily mean that it's simple to implement. There are a host of risks for colleges and universities in catering too narrowly to the needs of particular employers or preparing students too narrowly for particular jobs. Employers and jobs, as history tells us, come and go. Most people involved in higher education would undoubtedly agree that one of the objectives of a good, solid education is to prepare graduates to be adaptable, to be prepared for transitions in their careers that take them from one job to another, or even one industry to another. As Georgia Tech's McLaughlin suggested, the task is to provide students with skills for life, a life where circumstances, including industries, technologies, jobs, and interests all may change. So, yes, education providers could work more closely with employers to make sure that their offerings prepare students for a life of work, but likewise, as Drexel's Fry emphasizes, employers need to work with colleges and universities to define their needs in ways that speak not only to the near term but also to the long term and that recognize the importance for students to develop portable skills that can serve them well in many contexts over a lifetime.

In its 2012 report, McKinsey makes the need for this kind of two-way dialogue explicit, arguing that a genuine solution to the apparent gap between how these two constituencies define readiness requires a form of collaboration where education providers and employers "actively step into one another's worlds" so that the "education-to-employment journey is treated as a continuum."[21] The phrasing, again, is sensible, simple, and elegant, but the core idea is really quite radical. What would it mean to treat such a journey as a continuum? And what would it require of the parties involved—perhaps even something deeper than mere collaboration?

If we imagine education providers actively stepping into the world of work and employers actively stepping into the world of curriculum design, teaching, and experiential learning in order to engineer a more seamless pathway for students on their journey from education to employment, then we are picturing something quite new, something that could profoundly alter the way we think about designing, delivering, and assessing learning. To engineer such a continuum, we may well need to go beyond thinking about how education prepares students for work and begin thinking about how education reaches, informs, and develops a different kind of character: the *student-employee*, who is both a learner and a current or future worker. Effectively developing student-employees requires coupling instruction and work experience in a genuinely integrated fashion. Along such a continuum we would undoubtedly expect this kind of integration to be bidirectional, with the world of work and the expertise of employers reaching back into the classroom or lab or student meet-up to inform and develop what we might think of as the *employee-students'* engagement with their curriculum and its relevance to the applied context of a job task. In such a scenario, the task of evaluating students' success in achieving work readiness must necessarily be a shared responsibility between education providers and employers.

THE DIFFICULTY OF DEFINING
AND MEASURING WORK READINESS

For the time being, there is no canonical definition of work readiness against which institutions might assess their progress in effectively preparing work-ready graduates. But there is evidence that higher education leaders are groping toward one. For some, such as Purcell at Plymouth, achieving work readiness means parallel processing: "We embed employability throughout the curriculum from day one and we then continue to focus on developing the entrepreneurial skills of our students through academic courses as well as support, mentoring, and networking opportunities."[22] She argues that achieving educational and employment outcomes through coordinated effort requires a different kind of relationship with the student. "A key factor in our success," she notes, "has been to establish our unique 'students as partners' charter which, rather than a transactional relationship that places the student as a customer, we feel that we take joint responsibility with our students for their educational outcomes. This means that as well as supporting employment opportunities, whether through internships or placements, we recognize that we are preparing graduates for jobs that don't even exist yet and for a career that will be multidimensional and more akin to a career portfolio."

For Kenneth Freeman, dean of the School of Management at Boston University, the key to student success today is flexibility and creativity. Thus, Freeman argues that in addition to hard knowledge, students must possess certain soft skills and personality traits, including "social intelligence, passion, curiosity, optimism and, especially, common sense."[23] For Lee Newman, dean of Social and Behavioral Sciences at IE University in Spain, the task falls to companies "to formalize the inclusion of behavioral criteria" in their recruiting efforts, including "criteria such as self-awareness, mindfulness, self-control, and empathy."[24] For Fry, at Drexel, the key fact is that employers aren't just looking for critical thinkers: "What they really want are motivated employees who can apply that thinking to make decisions and solve problems creatively. Such 'practical knowledge' is about knowing how to listen, disagree, assert an opinion, interrupt, and change people's minds, all in the course of a workday."[25]

Many of these characteristics are, of course, difficult to measure—or at least more difficult to measure than, say, a student's performance on a multiple choice final exam. And it remains to be seen how faculty might actually set out to promote the development of these kinds of skills or traits in the classroom in a more intentional way. But there are worthy ideas here. Helping students to think about the relevance of a curriculum to their future employability from the very beginning of their studies is no doubt a good place to start, and conceiving of the student-institution relationship as a partnership designed to support the achievement of targeted academic and professional outcomes in a coordinated way may well improve on the sink-or-swim attitude that may still prevail among certain faculty at some institutions. Furthermore, teaching students to intentionally develop qualities such as mindfulness, inquisitiveness, assertiveness, empathy, self-awareness, motivation, curiosity, optimism, and resilience can only be a good thing—*if* instructors can help students recognize that these qualities count in a professional setting. Of course, the best way to help them to recognize this is to provide them with opportunities to be in a professional setting—whether through internships, apprenticeships, co-ops, or authentic problem-solving experiences—and, even more importantly, to challenge them to reflect on how qualities such as these, in combination with the technical skills and knowledge base they have built up, can aid them in contributing in a productive fashion in a particular professional setting.

If colleges and universities can work more closely with employers to develop and assess these kinds of capabilities, then we may well be moving closer to scaling a Drownproofing 2.0 model. But there are challenges that will have to be considered and obstacles that will have to be removed before such a model can be truly deployed at scale. Reengineering the education-to-employment pathway as a continuum will require radical change, including new behaviors on the part of both educators and employers in areas as diverse as curriculum design, delivery models (on campus, online, hybrid, in the workplace), and assessment. These are facets of higher education with well-established traditions, values, and expectations; proposals for change will prove attractive to some but misguided to others, and obstacles will inevitably have to be overcome—if they can be overcome—with persuasion, evidence, proven models, and well-designed plans for linking education to employability.

A SKILLS GAP OR A COLLABORATION GAP?

As the McKinsey data suggests, there may well be a disconnect between the way education providers perceive the work readiness of their students and the way employers view those students. Certainly, many CEOs have been quoted in the popular press bemoaning the "skills gap" and pointing to the shortcomings of a certain portion of recent college graduates as they seek to enter the workforce. It remains a point of public debate, however, whether such a thing as a skills gap really exists. The fact that this debate is even being aired may provide support to those who would counsel our college and university leaders not to be hasty in designing degree programs with particular industries, companies, or professional positions in mind.

Labor market guru Peter Cappelli, from the University of Pennsylvania's Wharton School, has cast doubt on the existence of a skills gap. In an August 2012 commentary in the *New York Times*, he argued that a skills gap fails to serve as an effective explanation for apparent labor shortages. In particular, he saw four problems with this characterization of the labor market challenge: first, organizations may simply not be offering fair market compensation for the talent they want; second, their hiring requirements may be too severe and misaligned with their real needs simply because it is a buyer's market; third, they may not be investing adequately in training of existing staff; and fourth, they may not be making significant enough efforts to partner with colleges and universities to define educational programs that meet their needs.[26]

In a July 2014 commentary, Walter Frick of the *Harvard Business Review* noted that "companies complain that there is a shortage of talent, economists counter that if that were true it would be evidenced by rising wages. With wages stagnant, where's the skills gap?"[27] Pointing to a just-released report from the Brookings Institution, "Still Searching: Job Vacancies and STEM Skills," Frick attempts to focus on a perhaps less complex claim: "there are very real skills shortages in certain fields, namely computers and health care."[28]

In the Brookings report Jonathan Rothwell compares pre- and postrecession rates of reposted job openings across a variety of industries. While job repostings generally rebounded after 2008, only the computer and health care sectors showed reposting rates by 2012 that were higher than they were prerecession. Based on this observation, Rothwell notes that "the relatively high levels of difficulty in filling job vacancies for computer and health care occupations appear to be as acute after the recession as before—a period of low unemployment and tight labor markets. Therefore, the contemporary relative shortage of work workers in these positions is especially severe."[29]

As Frick suggests, the argument about a skills gap may be academic. And both Cappelli and Rothwell make creditable points. Cappelli's argument illustrates how effectively addressing the challenges associated with developing the capabilities of future workers will require greater self-reflection on the part of employers and institutions of higher education alike, as well as closer cooperation between them. Rothwell's analysis suggests that certain industries are finding it harder to identify skilled talent. These are not incompatible assertions.

Boston University economist James Bessen views the debate somewhat differently, arguing that while it would be wrong to blame a shortage of skills for causing unemployment, as well as wrong to assert that the talent pool is not sufficiently educated (he notes that "too many workers may be overeducated"), he does believe there is a skills gap.[30] The problem, he says, is that skills demanded by the labor market can be difficult to measure, particularly if the skills in demand have to do with the effective use of new technologies. These skills are skills that "schools don't teach and that labor markets don't supply," according to Bessen. But, in his view, the difficulty associated with measuring these kinds of skills creates an opportunity, and undoubtedly that opportunity creates an occasion for schools and employers to collaborate in defining, measuring, and addressing whatever gaps exist. Indeed, even if the rhetoric about a purported skills gap may be overstated, that doesn't mean that education providers and employers wouldn't benefit from a collaborative effort to bring their respective resources to bear on particular local, regional, and national economic challenges. As Cappelli points out, however, that will require a capacity for self-reflection on the part of both parties.

Fortunately, we appear to find ourselves at just such a moment of self-reflection. Much as industry is looking to reduce inefficiencies and eliminate unnecessary spending to strengthen its output, American higher education institutions are engaging in a period of serious reflection with respect to their core competencies and value-added contributions to the growth and sustainability of local and regional economies as well as the sustainability of their own business models.

OVERCOMING THE EDUCATION AND TRAINING DIVIDE

Given the financial pressure that many institutions find themselves under, it's little wonder that they may be expecting employers (particularly corporate employers) to step up in a more pronounced fashion. There are certainly some within the higher education community who feel that corporations are not doing enough to support the professional development of their employees. Some even argue that employers are spending less on training than in the past and thus are leaving colleges and universities to shoulder the burden of providing this kind of professional development. The data, at an aggregate level, however, suggests otherwise. According to Bersin by Deloitte, a firm that tracks corporate training expenditures, domestic investments in corporate training have grown from a recent low of approximately $47 billion in 2009 to $70 billion in 2013, with double-digit growth over each of the last three years. That's not to say that corporations shouldn't be doing more to collaborate with higher education providers, of course—they should, particularly if we hope to arrive at a better matching of recent graduates to jobs. But raw spending does not appear to be a significant challenge. What may be more critical to examine is where and how corporations are making those investments—in particular, whether those investments are being made at the senior level or entry level. Universities that are willing to step forward to examine those questions with their corporate partners in the process of identifying more cost-effective and productive ways of sharing the education and professional development challenge may well find that benefits accrue to both parties.

An obstacle to these sorts of efforts, of course, is the way many within the higher education community view training and the way many within the employer community view apprenticeships. For educators, training is often seen as vocational, not educational. For some employers, apprenticeship programs may have similarly undesirable associations with blue collar trades. Although we might expect the focus on jobs and work readiness since the 2008 recession to have changed minds about training and apprenticeships, the problem may actually be worsening. Citing Department of Labor data, the *Wall Street Journal* noted that "formal programs that combine on-the-job learning with mentorships and classroom education fell 40 percent in the U.S. between 2003 and 2013."[31] Furthermore, "two-thirds of apprenticeship programs in the U.S. are in the construction industry, furthering a blue-collar image that stifles interest among young people and the employers who could create jobs for them." Other sources of anxiety for some employers are the association between apprenticeships and unions and the prospect "that employees will leave for better-paying jobs almost as soon as they've learned their required skills." It remains to be seen whether the Obama administration's funding initiatives to support employability can help ameliorate these anxieties for employers and education providers alike. While community colleges and their workforce development partners will no doubt remain eager to tap into these funding streams, action will be required from a more diverse set of institutions and employers for these programs to have an impact at scale.

LEARNING HOW TO TEACH ONLINE

Tucked within the Obama administration's numerous work readiness initiatives announced in the summer of 2014 is a $25 million program to support the development of an online skills academy.[32] On the same day the program was announced, the California State University System announced that it would be closing its systemwide distance education portal, Cal State Online, which was launched two years ago with the stated objective of enrolling 250,000 students, in favor of a more distributed model, where each Cal State institution will continue to develop its own programs with support from the chancellor's office.[33] Given that higher education institutions have been delivering courses and degree programs online since the 1990s, and taking into the consideration the celebratory reception that massive open online courses (MOOCs) received just a few years ago, one might think that online learning is old hat by now, and thus the prospects for an online learning initiative to foster work readiness would be well-positioned to succeed. Indeed, according to the National Center for Education Statistics, more than 5.5 million students—more than a quarter of all postsecondary students—took an online course in 2012.[34]

But as the Cal State news suggests, there's been some evidence of a backlash against online learning in the last year or two. Over that time we've witnessed faculty rebelling against online learning initiatives at institutions as diverse as Harvard,

Duke, Rutgers, and San Jose State, to name just a few.[35] In the latter case, faculty rallied to resist the use of Udacity courses on campus, while Duke faculty made the decision to withdraw from the 2U-sponsored Semester Online consortium, and Rutgers' Graduate School faculty voted to block the university's planned rollout of online degree programs through its partnership with Pearson, the same company Cal State partnered with for its online portal. Udacity, 2U, and Pearson are all for-profit companies, and in some quarters within higher education there is a negative association linking online learning to crass commercialism. If online learning does represent an opportunity to address challenges associated with fostering employability, then this perceived linkage will have to be overcome.

Of course, while some faculty have expressed concerns about the involvement of for-profit companies in supporting institutional efforts to design, market, and deliver courses and programs online, others have also sometimes expressed concerns about administrator overreach. At the heart of both of these complaints is a concern about the role of faculty in governance of the institution and its mission. Notwithstanding the twenty-year history of online learning in U.S. higher education, significant issues have still not been settled to everyone's satisfaction. Thus, while online learning undoubtedly will continue to play a role in supporting employability, fostering work readiness, and assisting in the professional development of working adults, there is still much political ground for many colleges and universities to cover when it comes to managing their online initiatives. Today, the issue is seldom a question of whether to be online; instead, it's more frequently a question of how to be online, a question that encompasses not only governance matters but also matters of leadership and organizational structure. Even institutions that have been active online for a number of years are still facing important questions in these areas as they seek to bring their efforts to scale. Thus, as colleges and universities look to partner with employers to forge a more seamless pathway from education to work, issues related to the governance and management of online learning will undoubtedly require further consideration.

MODULARIZING CURRICULUM

One of the great challenges, as well as one of the great benefits, associated with online learning is that it often requires faculty to rethink how they teach. This can become especially challenging when institutions strive for world-class production values in their online courses and programs or incorporate new technologies such as adaptive learning solutions. In essence, good online learning may require faculty to deconstruct their curriculum before rebuilding it in ways tailored to this different medium. This kind of disassembly of a curriculum can be time consuming and frustrating for faculty who are used to charting their own path and making adjustments to syllabi on the fly. Some faculty find this kind of challenge liberating, and later report that their classroom teaching has been reinvigorated as a result; other faculty simply feel that too much effort is required to build good online courses and too little control is offered in return. Thus, the inflexibility of the curriculum may remain a speed bump as institutions strive to develop more market-responsive degree and certificate offerings to support work readiness and professional development.

Yet, this is not solely a challenge associated with online learning. The burgeoning movement in competency-based education brings with it many of the same challenges, as curriculum must be broken down into smaller units before being repackaged in new ways. Consider one of the cases highlighted by McKinsey. AMTEC (Automotive Manufacturing Training and Education Collective) is a multistate effort to forge workforce development collaborations between auto manufacturers and technical and community colleges that is supported by the National Science Foundation (NSF) and the Kentucky Community and Technical College System. "To develop the AMTEC curriculum," McKinsey reports, "high-performing technicians (not managers) from several auto companies outlined every task they performed and the competencies required for each."[36] Based on these competencies, employers and education providers "worked together to distill all this information into a curriculum composed of 60 three-to-eight-week study modules spanning 110 core competencies, with each module focusing on specific skill sets." An important feature of the curriculum, McKinsey notes, is its modular design, "which gives students more flexibility in combining, sequencing, or spreading out their learning as required." This kind of modularization is difficult for many institutions to manage, and yet refashioning existing curricula to meet the needs of growing numbers of current and future workers may well require similar levels of invention and flexibility.

FROM COMPETITION TO CO-OPETITION

The AMTEC consortium represents an interesting model for a geographically distributed but industrially focused collaboration at scale. Among the numerous challenges associated with this form of collaboration—not the least of which would be adequate funding and identifying shared interests in undertaking such a complex project—is the prospect of collaborating with competitors. AMTEC was designed to foster not only college-to-industry partnerships but also college-to-college and industry-to-industry partnerships. Projects like this require competitors to engage in new ways, and the resulting *co-opetition* can be difficult for many organizations to pull off. If successful, these kinds of geographically organized projects can bring multiple participants into cooperative arrangements that are anything but a zero-sum game.

Michael Porter argues that place continues to play a significant role in economic development, even in a globalized economy, despite what one might imagine about the myriad choices for developing a global supply chain. He points to Hollywood as one example of an organic, geographically situated cluster comprised of a range of interrelated and interdependent industries and support services. He defines clusters of this sort as "geographic concentrations of interconnected companies and institutions" encompassing "an array of linked industries" as well as "governmental and other institutions—such as universities, standards-setting agencies, think tanks, vocational training providers, and trade associations—that provide specialized training, education, information, research, and technical support."[37] A cluster, Porter argues, is "an alternative way of organizing the value chain."

Thomas Kochan, David Finegold, and Paul Osterman outline how something like Porter's notion of the cluster can be brought to bear on the challenges associated with the so-called skills gap. They write, "Credible data on what businesses spend on training are scarce, but companies are known to target HR investments first when cutting budgets. Many firms fear that if they invest in training on their own, competitors that don't make similar investments will lure away their workers."[38] Kochan and his coauthors argue that the remedy to this challenge is to establish "collaborative programs that involve multiple employers in a region or industry sector, educational institutions, and other players such as unions and governments." In this way, the risks faced by individual organizations in investing in talent development are shared with other organizations in the region and thereby diminished as the collective investments made through these collaborations benefit all participants. Seen this way, co-opetition promises to generate a return in exchange for the risk involved. Of course, there is risk. And institutions that enter into such arrangements without clear plans for generating a return or a well-designed exit strategy if expected returns do not materialize will face the risk of potentially losing market share or otherwise compromising their positioning in the local market.

But there is, perhaps, an even bigger threat posed by sitting on the side lines: the threat of substitutes emerging. If, as FSG argues, companies are assuming responsibilities formerly associated with colleges and universities, what is to prevent them from competing directly with institutions? The simple and largely persuasive answer is accreditation. Only accredited institutions have the authority to grant degrees, and that, more often than not, is what employees and future employees really want—not just the education, not just the skill building, but the degree or certificate as well. Currently, colleges and universities have a lock on accreditation. And up to now no organization has been successful at creating demand for a different kind of education credential at scale, notwithstanding the many "open badges" initiatives in recent years.[39]

But perhaps accreditation isn't the insurmountable barrier it has so long appeared to be. Consider the announcement by Udacity, the for-profit learning platform company, and AT&T to collaborate in offering a different kind of educational product: the nanodegree.[40] Sebastian Thrun, the Stanford University computer scientist who founded Udacity in 2012, recently characterized his company's partnership with AT&T to deliver online courses in basic programming for $200 a month as being "like a university built by industry."[41] Eduardo Porter characterizes the Udacity offering as delivering training in "a narrow set of skills that can be clearly applied to a job, providing learners with a bite-size chunk of knowledge and an immediate motivation to acquire it. It may not offer all the advantages of a liberal arts education, but it could offer a plausible path to young men and women who may not have the time, money or skill to make it through a four-year or even a two-year degree."[42] Of course, Udacity is not alone in attempting to provide a commercial solution to a long-standing education problem. (A handful of other efforts by for-profit companies to address the work-readiness education needs of individuals not currently being met by colleges and universities are examined in chapter 2.) The proliferation of such organizations is interesting and bears some attention for what it may suggest about opportunities for easing the college-to-work transition for many, as well as for what it may suggest about possible improvements to institutional-industry partnerships. But it will be some time before these companies or their successors will be able to establish anything like a genuine market alternative to the accredited college degree.

Be that as it may, colleges and universities and their employer partners cannot afford to stand still if they wish to avoid the risk of falling quickly behind. The Drownproofing 2.0 imperative demands a response, and innovation will be a key ingredient of that response, particularly as universities and industry partners seek to prepare the next generation of talent to tackle some of today's most pressing employment needs. The partnership between the University of Maryland and Northrop

Grumman around cyber security is one example, and IBM's partnership with Ohio State around data analytics is another. But even these relationships will need to continue to develop to become truly game changing. As Jim Spohrer, director of IBM Global University Programs, put it, "For the partnerships to grow in sophistication, both universities and industry are going to have to change."[43]

EMPLOYABILITY AND THE HIGHER EDUCATION VALUE CHAIN

The motivations for change seem clear enough. Employers want to reduce the cost of recruiting, and they want their recruiting investments to produce more effective outcomes, which means getting the right talent for the right job and hiring individuals whose talents can be developed and adapted to the needs of a particular industry, organization, and profession. Universities want to demonstrate that academic outcomes have a bearing on professional outcomes, and they want to attract the best students possible in part by demonstrating that they can introduce those students to attractive professional opportunities. Deeper collaboration between employers and institutions will undoubtedly improve the chances of success for both parties as well as for the other key stakeholders, such as students, their parents, and the communities which the institutions and employers serve.

To that end, fostering work readiness and smoothing out the college-to-work transition is an important challenge for both sectors to take up, and our contemporary economic challenges create timely new incentives for higher education institutions and employers from industry, government, and the nonprofit arena to collaborate more closely in addressing that challenge through a wide range of means. As Plymouth University's Wendy Purcell argues, institutions can enhance the value they deliver to their students if they treat their students' future employment as a matter of concern from day one, rather than as a matter for the career services office to tackle once the student reaches the spring term of his senior year. To achieve this, institutions need to be thinking about employability well before the students even arrive.

For example, growing numbers of institutions are becoming increasingly sophisticated in their decision making about curriculum development, mapping the curriculum of proposed new degree or certificate programs to the labor gaps in particular geographic regions where they have students. This is where data companies like Burning Glass and EMSI can provide colleges and universities with almost real-time information about job demand in particular markets. Of course, institutions can also turn to their numerous industry advisory boards for perspective. But the challenge is to make such input matter. It's one thing to call on industry advisory boards to corroborate curriculum decisions, and it's another thing to invite representatives of the employer community in at the drawing board stage to inform a better understanding of the local or regional market needs and to provide input to early-stage decisions regarding the purpose of new program offerings.

Additionally, institutions can turn to the employer community to better understand how the success or failure of past graduates from existing programs can inform improvements to curriculum. Assessment of student outcomes will no doubt increasingly become a matter of shared concern for education providers and employers, and the closer the collaboration between institutions and employers regarding these forms of assessment, the more powerful and consequential such information will be to the design of new degree and certificate offerings.

While problem-based learning is by no means a new concept, the kind of closer collaboration between institutions and employers I anticipate here presents an opportunity to think more deeply about how to integrate genuinely real-world, problem-based learning—or, as David Angel put it, "authentic problem-solving situations"—into the curriculum, and not just in the form of a capstone project for a degree and not just once in the context of a given course but potentially on an even more frequent and routine basis throughout a given student's course of study.

The opportunity to produce real-world work product in a high-stakes setting—producing a design project or a business plan or a financial analysis that will actually be used to inform current business decisions within an employer partner organization—can be further augmented if institutions can think wisely about how to put technology to effective use in delivering increasingly personalized, adaptive, and outcomes-oriented educational programs and courses. Adaptive learning companies such as Knewton, LearnSmart, CogBooks, and Cerego offer new ways of providing students and instructors with real-time feedback on the students' progress through a curriculum while also allowing students the opportunity to demonstrate mastery of discrete chunks of that curriculum in ways that allow some to move forward more quickly and others to move more slowly through the most challenging portions of their course materials until they feel that they genuinely understand the key concepts. As with online learning, however, weaving together a modular, adaptive curriculum can require more design time up front, and faculty must be willing to invest that time, aided by instructional designers, if the potential for these tools to impact student performance is to be realized.

With virtually all industries and their supply chains globalized to one degree or another, it is also important that colleges and universities consider how to bring students into contact with other educational and professional cultures around the world, thereby fostering increased global fluency by means of diverse sorts of international educational experiences. Being international can mean many things, of course, ranging from the diversity of the institution's campus-based student body to the internationalization of the curriculum to the opportunity to study or work abroad as a component of students' degree programs. Being an effectively international institution means connecting students to global markets that are relevant to their courses of study and that open up possible pathways for future professional work. Thus, relationships with employers in market will inevitably be key to making these educational experiences academically relevant and professionally promising.

As Drexel's Fry underscores, it is increasingly critical that institutions and employers collaborate to support the development of meaningful opportunities for experiential learning, cooperative education, apprenticeships, internships, and other real-world professional experiences. This is, of course, easier said than done, and we have already seen that apprenticeships, for example, are far less common here in the United States than in other countries around the world. Co-op programs are resource intensive, and it takes years of work to develop the relationships with employers necessary to support a co-op program at scale. Yet, growing numbers of institutions are promoting their experiential learning offerings to prospective students and parents, and this kind of value proposition is something we should expect to see more of in the years ahead—even if the difference between claiming to offer it and actually offering it can sometimes be significant.

Assuming that greater numbers of institutions, students, and employers will be offering and participating in experiential learning programs, it will be increasingly important for education providers and employers to synchronize their efforts to assess student performance in those settings. This will require far greater collaboration around assessment than we have traditionally seen between institutions and employers. Competency-based education models may suggest one path to arriving at a lingua franca for academic assessment and professional performance measurement, but even there education providers and employers will have to agree on which competencies matter and how they are defined and assessed. As the AMTEC case demonstrates, this kind of work will necessarily represent no small undertaking. If such a system of assessment could be developed, however, to function effectively in both domains, then institutions utilizing such a system of assessment would be at an advantage in demonstrating the success of their graduates as well as in predicting the employability of their current students.

Employers can also play a valued role by serving as mentors and coaches to students seeking to better understand how their capabilities, skills, and interests align with particular professional opportunities. Employers, both in group and one-on-one contexts, can provide students with practical perspective on the skills needed to succeed in their industry and the qualities necessary in individuals seeking to build a successful career in that professional context.

The opportunities for institutional and employer collaboration extend along the length of the higher education value chain—from identifying market needs to program design, from problem-based learning to experiential learning opportunities, from assessment to mentoring models. Ultimately, the institution's career services office should play a key role in these partnerships, not only by helping students gain exposure to professional opportunities and benefit from guidance on how best to position their value to the market but also by assisting employers in gaining exposure to the students whose backgrounds and capabilities best match their recruiting needs. Done well, employability should not only be a matter of consideration for students and their institutions from day one, it should be a consideration that carries forward to the moment when students make that transition from the world of education to the world of work.

EDUCATION TO EMPLOYMENT—OR, LEARN-CERTIFY-DEPLOY, LEARN-CERTIFY-DEPLOY

A futurist, someone once said, is a person who talks about the present to the 98 percent of us who live in the past. In some important respects, the deeper collaboration so many seek between education providers and employers—including governments, policy makers, economists, students, parents, employers, and institutions themselves—is already under way. But there is still some road to travel to realize the full potential for these collaborations, and there are numerous visions to guide our goal setting as we move down that road.

Students, for example, have their own thoughts. A recent poll conducted by Zogby Analytics in collaboration with Laureate Education reported that 41 percent of more than twenty thousand students surveyed in twenty-one countries anticipate that in the future "students will be able to earn credits and certificates throughout their careers, instead of cramming college into a two- or four-year stint. In other words, they say, students of the future will get practical training on an as-needed basis."[44]

Institutions have their own visions, as well, and they are by no means necessarily at odds with the views expressed by these students. The *Chronicle of Higher Education* recently conducted an interview with a University of Pennsylvania Wharton School professor Christian Terwiesch, who foresees a day when Wharton "eventually might have to provide chunks of its curriculum on demand over a student's whole career . . . rather than during a two year stretch at the beginning."[45] Terwiesch envisions a future where students may spend close to a year on campus to experience the benefits of building a network and then enter the workforce and enroll on a subscription basis to have access to a library of just-in-time education resources in the form of an "online 'minicourse,'" meaning that the model shifts from one of "learn-learn-learn-certify-wait-wait-wait-deploy" to one of "learn-certify-deploy, learn-certify-deploy."

Ultimately, the life skills that students need most today and tomorrow may extend beyond the ability to create their own job. Indeed, the next iteration of Drownproofing might incorporate the capacity to train students to tailor their own educational programs and delivery models on an as-needed basis throughout their working lives.

2

INNOVATORS, ENTREPRENEURS, AND THE THREAT OF SUBSTITUTES

Today, numerous forces at work in the higher education market—economic forces, consumer forces, competitive forces, regulatory forces, and so on—call out for an institutional response. Some schools respond out of dire necessity: enrollments are slipping, revenue is compromised, expenses are rising. Other institutions see in a moment of economic turbulence an occasion to define a new niche for themselves and an opportunity to establish a more distinctive value proposition by serving a particular set of students. Still other institutions may be relatively content with both the state of their finances and their brands, and thus they can afford the luxury of exploring new areas patiently to see what benefits might emerge from experimentation.

It's possible to see the Drownproofing 2.0 imperative playing out in all of these ways across the diversity of U.S. institutions of higher learning. There has been some significant innovation around the theme of employability in recent years, much of it emerging at the margins of the higher education community, at institutions that are not well-known and which do not possess national brands, though a focus on the education-to-employment transition and work readiness is now on the cusp of becoming mainstream.

Of course, for some—particularly parents and students, but also legislators, employers, and even some institutions—innovation in this domain can't come soon enough. As a result, colleges and universities now find themselves not just contending with their peers to provide more compelling employability solutions but also competing with a burgeoning community of entrepreneurs and investors, some working in partnership with startups and others working with a handful of the world's largest companies to develop employability solutions of their own.

Before examining the current state of innovation among a small number of research universities, I want to pan back and look at the wider arena of innovation around employability among a more diverse set of institutions as well as a variety of companies. These organizations may well have useful lessons they can pass along to the broader higher education community about fostering work readiness and creating a more seamless path from education to employment.

COMPETENCY-BASED EDUCATION MODELS

Institutions as diverse as Western Governors University, Southern New Hampshire University (SNHU), the State University of New York (SUNY) system, the University of Wisconsin system, Capella University, Rensselaer Polytechnic Institute, Middlebury College, Harvard Business School (HBS), and many others have explored new ways of fostering work readiness in recent years. Some of these institutions—Western Governors,

SNHU, Wisconsin, and Capella among them—are focusing on competency-based education (CBE) models that attempt to align curriculum and assessment more directly to the skill requirements of particular jobs and professions. Others are focusing on experiential learning and professional coaching, including SUNY, Middlebury, and Harvard Business School. For yet another group of institutions the focus has been on curricular collaborations, as in the case of Rensselaer, which has recently partnered with IBM around the delivery of courses in cognitive computing.[1]

The fledgling movement in competency-based education got a tremendous boost in the spring of 2013 when the U.S. Department of Education announced that federal financial aid could now be awarded to students based on their mastery of skills or competencies in addition to the traditional metric, the credit hour. Southern New Hampshire University was the first institution to be approved for eligibility to award financial aid for a form of CBE called *direct assessment*. Through its College for America division, SNHU developed first an associate degree program and then a bachelor's degree to be delivered via self-paced online instruction that assesses students on their ability to demonstrate mastery in 120 areas of competency.[2] In other words, the College for America program allows students to effectively test out of certain courses if they already possess the experience necessary to demonstrate mastery through the assessments or to move through courses at their own pace until they are prepared to demonstrate mastery and progress. The cost is $2,500 a year for both degrees, making it possible for an individual to potentially earn a bachelor's degree for $10,000 or less.[3] In fact, just a few short months after the Department of Education approved SNHU's program, College for America's first graduate, a twenty-one-year-old working for ConAgra Foods in Troy, Ohio, completed the associate degree program in fewer than one hundred days.[4]

Of course, SNHU was not the first institution to allow students to test out of particular courses based on prior knowledge and experience. Prior learning assessment (PLA) has been a common practice in higher education for decades, but it has been a marginal activity, typically confined to divisions of continuing education and primarily in service of degree completion programs targeting working adults seeking to come back to higher education after long spells in the workforce. The purpose of PLA is to recognize the professional knowledge and achievements of working adults through the awarding of commensurate academic credit, but PLA was never designed to replace coursework altogether. To the contrary, the number of credits an individual might earn through PLA is capped at some level. For example, a community college might permit no more than 30 PLA credits to be applied to a 60-credit associate degree program, and a four-year institution might permit no more than 60 PLA credits to be applied to a 120-credit bachelor's degree program, though in some cases a greater proportion of PLA credit may be allowed. SNHU's College for America represents a significant break from the PLA tradition insofar as it makes it possible—at least theoretically—for a student to test her way to an entire associate or bachelor's degree.

Nor was SNHU the first institution to offer self-paced online courses designed to allow students to demonstrate academic mastery of curricula. Western Governors University has long offered self-paced online degree programs through which students can demonstrate mastery of content through test taking. Prior to the Department of Education's approval of the awarding of federal financial aid for such programs, institutions had to map competencies to credits if they wished their students to be eligible for federal financial aid programs, and this has been the approach adopted by Western Governors. SNHU's program represents an advancement in competency-based models inasmuch as it was the first institution to be eligible to award federal financial aid to students whose learning would be measured through direct assessment of competencies rather than on the basis of the credit hour.

The for-profit Capella University, which delivers its programs exclusively online, was similarly approved by the Department of Education shortly after SNHU, and then followed by Northern Arizona University and the University of Wisconsin system.[5] So far only SNHU and Capella have been successful at getting their programs approved both by the U.S. Department of Education and their regional accreditors.[6] While some other institutions have attempted to gain approval from their regional accreditors, not all have been successful, suggesting that not every accreditor is confident about CBE models just yet. But the CBE movement received a boost in the summer of 2014 when the U.S. Department of Education announced the establishment of a demonstration program that permits a growing number of institutions to award federal financial aid for CBE programs. As many as 350 institutions are reported to already offer or are seeking to offer such programs.[7]

It remains to be seen, of course, how the broader higher education community offering traditional, credit-hour-based degrees elects to handle transfer students with competency-based credits or credentials, particularly as no standard framework currently exists to guide institutions in determining which competencies align with which courses at their own institutions. In the absence of such a framework, competency-based credits and credentials may make it more difficult for students to move between institutions and may thereby slow the advancement of those students' educational attainment.

THE EXPANSION OF EXPERIENTIAL LEARNING OPPORTUNITIES AND BRIDGE PROGRAMS

In parallel with those institutions leading the CBE movement, a number of other colleges and universities have been promoting their experiential learning opportunities or professional coaching services. In early 2014, for example, the State University of New York system announced an expansion of its SUNY Works program, which aims to support cooperative education initiatives, internships, service learning, and community service opportunities in partnership with Fortune 500 companies operating in the state.[8] Kaitlin Gambrill, the assistant vice chancellor for Strategic Planning and University Advancement in the SUNY system, said in the weeks following this announcement that "this whole conversation wasn't happening more than ten years ago. Nobody cared what happened when you left school. You just paid your bill and you left. Now I think there are examples that are harder and harder to ignore of different sectors integrating with each other. The whole world of higher education is changing, and we can't stop it."[9]

What makes the SUNY initiative significant is, first, the scale of the system itself—encompassing sixty-four distinct campuses across one of the most populous states in the nation—and, second, the boldness of the effort, underscored by Chancellor Nancy Zimpher's effort to engage every Fortune 500 company operating in the state in collaborating through SUNY Works. In other respects, SUNY has been relatively slow to get into the game. Cooperative education, or co-op, programs, which typically take the form of semester-length, paid professional experiences, have been up and running at some institutions for more than a century, including schools like the University of Cincinnati, Northeastern University, and Drexel University. The SUNY system's leadership seems determined to make up for lost time, however, and its actions could provoke other institutions and state systems to follow suit.

Another emergent subgenre of experiential learning has been the bridge program, which typically aims, through a few weeks of coaching, to augment liberal arts students' education with an applied curriculum related to business. Dartmouth College's Tuck School of Business has been running the Tuck Business Bridge Program since 1997.[10] Tuck serves a very different audience with its $10,000 summer program than does SNHU with its $10,000 bachelor's degree through College for America.[11] The offerings respond to different needs in the market, and the Tuck model has been implemented at a number of other universities with strong business programs targeting similar audiences. One is Vanderbilt, where the Vanderbilt Summer Business Institute was founded in 2004 to provide business education to undergraduates studying a variety of majors.[12]

But other sorts of institutions have seen opportunity here as well. In 2008, Middlebury College, well known for its liberal arts and language programs, launched its own bridge program, MiddCORE, unaided by the presence of an established business school.[13] The four-week summer program costs $9,500 and aims to help liberal arts students develop fundamental business skills and more effectively position them in the labor market following graduation.

Other liberal arts institutions have followed suit, albeit with different funding models.[14] Northland College in Ashland, Wisconsin, has recently launched, and pays for, a career bridge semester for recent graduates. St. Lawrence University in Canton,

New York, offers its Career Connections "boot camp," a two-day intersession program for sophomores that seeks to improve students' resume writing and interviewing skills, among other things. As with Northland, St. Lawrence's program is free to the students, though it costs the university $20,000 to serve 110 second-year students. As Geoffrey Falen, the Career Connections director, observed, when institutions are charging tuition of $50,000 or more, it's critical to have something to point to in order to answer the question many parents are asking—"What is my kid going to do . . . Where is the return on educational investment?"[15] It remains to be seen how the Northland and St. Lawrence programs perform with respect to providing answers to questions such as those, whether parents find the answers sufficiently satisfying, or whether the funding models will remain unchanged going forward. Clearly institutions of various stripes serving different constituencies will have to arrive at their own pricing strategies and business models to support their employability offerings.

EMPLOYABILITY AND ONLINE LEARNING

Of course, it isn't only the small liberal arts institution that is asking how to better prepare students for the world of work and to more effectively connect them to the labor market. Institutions with global brands, such as MIT and Harvard Business School, are examining these questions as well. As Bob Karp, a senior Industrial Liaison Program (ILP) officer at MIT, said, "There's no question that universities can benefit from being better informed about the things industry is looking for—the problems they're trying to solve, the capabilities that employees are going to need to have. Likewise, industry should be better informed about what's happening on this side of the fence.

It should be two-way communication."[16] MIT's Industrial Liaison Program is a membership organization with more than two hundred participating companies from around the world. The university provides its members with a variety of services to connect them to MIT faculty, encourage research collaboration, and ultimately benefit MIT students. Karp said, "We're here as an intermediary to make it easier for the members to know what's happening on campus, who's doing it, whether it resonates with them, and to get them some face time with faculty to learn more about it. We also organize regular conferences with MIT faculty, provide customized executive briefings, and offer many other specialized services." While enhancing the employability of MIT graduates is not the stated mission of the ILP, students can benefit significantly from the relationships the office develops. "Does the ILP lead to collaboration and sponsored research? Absolutely it does," said Karp. "And that research often results in graduate students or postdocs, and often undergraduates, being hired into projects. And some of them get hired into these companies, based on the work they're doing on these projects and having had the chance to get to know the companies and their problems."

Karp also pointed to the potential of edX, MIT's online collaboration with Harvard University and a number of other institutions to promote MOOCs, as a significant vehicle for delivering value to MIT's students and industry partners while also capturing valuable data on student learning that can meaningfully inform online as well as on-campus pedagogies. "EdX will transform residential education," Karp stated. "It absolutely will not do away with it. There are many benefits to living on campus—the whole experience socially for young people growing up, and also face time with the faculty, and research is hugely important. But I think we can make it better if we do a really good job of delivering some of the redundant basics with technology like edX."[17]

Harvard Business School has been keeping an eye on edX and appears to be more explicitly interested in the potential for online learning to provide new means for helping students transition from education to employment or strengthen their employability. In March 2014 HBS announced the launch of HBX, its own online learning venture, offering fee-based courses targeting students studying the liberal arts and technical disciplines as well as executives and other HBS alumni who seek access to fundamental business courses.[18] Its CORe (Credential of Readiness) offering is priced at $1,500 for a sequence of three courses, though its Web site warns that prices could rise in the future.[19] From the HBS perspective, what's particularly important about HBX is that it is designed to support the school's well-known case model for business education, and the new organization is eager to distinguish its fee-based courses from free MOOCs of the sort edX offers, which, like the free online courses from other MOOC providers, typically suffer 90–95 percent drop-out rates. "We don't want tourists," said Jana Kierstead, HBX's executive director. "Our goal is to be very credible to employers."[20]

ENTREPRENEURS AND INVESTORS
ARE TACKLING EMPLOYABILITY TOO

Witnessing the growing level of activity in the area of employability from such diverse institutions is certainly encouraging, yet colleges and universities are by no means the only organizations that have been paying attention to the challenges associated with the so-called skills gap or demonstrating concern about the work readiness of recent graduates—or taking action to address those problems. Indeed, fueled by public concern about the state of the economy, government calls for greater transparency regarding the return on individuals' higher education investments, and private investors pouring substantial flows of venture capital into the ed tech industry, dozens and dozens of startup companies have emerged in recent years to supplement—or, in some cases, substitute for—traditional colleges and universities.

According to CB Insights, education technology financings totaled more than $1.1 billion in 2012.[21] In 2013, the firm reported, investments in education technology grew to $1.25 billion, and in the first quarter of 2014 alone education companies raised $559 million more in capital. Those are significant sums of money, providing for-profit companies with resources well beyond the grasp of the vast majority of colleges and universities.

Consider a few examples. The experiential learning and professional coaching company Koru raised $4.35 million from Maveron, Battery Ventures, First Round Capital, and Andreessen Horowitz in the fall of 2013.[22] The coding training provider General Assembly raised $35 million in 2014 from Institutional Venture Partners, which, combined with the company's earlier rounds of funding, brought its total capital raised to just under $50 million.[23] The Minerva Project, a startup and a self-proclaimed "elite university," raised $25 million in seed funding from Benchmark Capital in 2012.[24] Of course, education companies seeking to address the work readiness challenges faced by today's recent graduates need more than money to be successful. They must also provide valuable new services if they hope to have a significant impact on the challenges associated with employability and if they intend to achieve sustainability for their own organizations. Of course, they also need a clear value proposition.

One of the benefits of starting a business from scratch is that entrepreneurs are not beholden to traditional models; they are free to combine value propositions in ways that may well differ from those of their institutional partners or competitors. Thus, we see startup companies bringing to market interesting new combinations of career services, mentoring resources, recruiting services, and social networking. It will be interesting to see how these entrepreneurial ventures, with their innovative combination of services, impact traditional institutions in their efforts to assist students in making the transition from education to employment, and in particular whether those companies succeed in delivering a more valuable service that institutions might ultimately adopt or whether they provide a template for an approach to career services that colleges and universities themselves may attempt to emulate and adapt to their own purposes. In the long term, there may be little benefit accrued to institutions that elect a third approach—which would be to do nothing.

STARTUP BRIDGE PROGRAMS

One of the most direct attempts to address the "skills gap" is being made by a small but growing number of companies delivering professional coaching services and experiential learning and internship opportunities.

The Fullbridge Program, founded in Cambridge, Massachusetts, in 2010 by Peter Olson, the former CEO of Random House, and Candice Carpenter Olson, the founder and former

CEO of iVillage, is a case in point.[25] The Fullbridge model is, in some respects, similar to Tuck's Bridge Program or MiddCORE. It offers multiweek programs ranging from 60 to 160 hours in an intensive boot camp model. The programs are designed to aid liberal arts students, as well as other audiences, in developing the soft and hard skills necessary to succeed in the job market. Program prices range from $1,500 to $7,500 for individual students, and bulk pricing models are being made available for employers and institutions that seek to incorporate Fullbridge services into their training organizations or student services functions. Corporate partners include Google, Patagonia, and Oracle; college and university clients include Harvard Law School, Wesleyan University, and Bowdoin.[26] In the summer of 2014 Fullbridge announced a partnership with Concordia University at Chicago to deliver an accredited graduate certificate program in business fundamentals for veterans transitioning to private-sector jobs, with tuition set at $8,882 for the five-week training course.[27] The Fullbridge case points to the interesting array of positions that for-profit companies of this type might assume relative to traditional colleges and universities. In some respects, Fullbridge may appear to compete with traditional institutions' bridge programs. Yet, some institutions may elect to purchase Fullbridge's services for their own students, while others may partner with Fullbridge to jointly serve particular segments of the market, such as veterans.

The Startup Institute, another kind of bridge program, offers an eight-week curriculum to help individuals prepare for work in a startup organization. It explicitly positions its offering as an adjunct to a college degree program rather than as a service that might be embedded within an academic context and exhibits no interest in partnering with institutions to deliver its services. The company's fees vary by geography, with prices of $4,750 in Boston and Chicago, $5,250 in New York City, and £3,000 in the United Kingdom.[28]

In 2013 Koru, an organization combining some of the qualities of both Fullbridge and Startup Institute, was launched in Seattle by Kristen Hamilton and Josh Jarrett. Koru also sets out to help liberal arts students develop their professional potential and find a more direct route into the workforce, particularly in attractive, relatively young companies. This newer entrant to the employability market distinguishes itself in part by incorporating internships at Seattle area companies such as Zulily, PayScale, and REI into its programs, as well as real-world, team-based work projects undertaken on behalf of its employer partners. Student tuition is $2,750 for a four-week program.[29] In the Koru model, students spend about a third of their time working inside real companies, and, much as in a traditional co-op program, these experiential learning opportunities provide both students and employers with the opportunity to observe one another closely en route to assessing the potential for a fit as a full-time hire.[30] In this way, Koru attempts to play a more direct role in assisting its students in making the transition from education to employment. Like Fullbridge, Koru has institutional partners that incorporate its services into their own student affairs and career services offerings, including institutions such as Brown University, Georgetown University, and Williams College.[31] Perhaps in response to the emergence of this new competitor, Fullbridge has recently moved to incorporate internships into its program offerings.[32]

While both Fullbridge and Koru represent interesting new ventures in the employability domain and offer potentially powerful benefits to their institutional and employer partners as well as their enrollees, they are not the first organizations to bring internships to their college and university partners' students. Dream Careers, formerly known as University of Dreams, traces its roots to 2000.[33] In 2010 the company acquired Career Explorations, a high school internship provider, and today Dream Careers operates both high school and college internship programs in diverse professional disciplines, reportedly working with students at more than five hundred colleges and universities annually and connecting them to three thousand employer partners around the world.[34]

Another, perhaps even less traditional, take on the experiential learning category, and one with a quite different financial model, is Black Mountain SOLE, founded in 2012 in Black Mountain, North Carolina. Black Mountain SOLE calls itself "the world's first 'self-organized learning environment' (SOLE) for higher education" and offers students the opportunity to design their own educational programs in the context of workshops, communities of practice, service projects, and more augmented by MOOCs and other do-it-yourself learning methods—tuition free.[35] The organization raised $5 million in the spring of 2013, though its future business model remains unclear.[36]

REIMAGINING CAREER SERVICES

Alongside these coaching and experiential learning organizations there is another class of for-profit venture in the education-to-employment marketplace that takes a less hands-on approach to assisting recent graduates as they seek to land career opportunities. Some of the companies in this category offer services at no cost to individual job seekers, while others charge fees ranging from a few dollars to over a thousand dollars. In many respects, these companies seek to supplement traditional college and university career services functions through Web-based self-service offerings that allow individuals to network with mentors or prospective employers, promote their educational accomplishments, exhibit real-world work product, or even participate in competitions sponsored by employers seeking talent.

Founded by a former head of marketing for Google, Sanjeev Agrawal, Collegefeed is a case in point. It provides a free online service that aims to make recent graduates' transitions from education to employment easier by aggregating resources and connecting them to more than five hundred companies as well as to one another.[37] Collegefeed makes money by charging companies for customized access to "feeds," or reports, on the students in its database and by permitting companies to brand themselves on the Collegefeed site.[38] Collegefeed also serves institutions such as Carnegie Mellon University, Cal Poly San Luis Obispo, University of Southern California, and others, providing supplementary career services resources to their students and analytics capabilities to their client institutions to assist them in better understanding their students' job search efforts.[39] In this way, the company not only equips students and recent graduates to take a more hands-on approach to managing their own job searches, but it also enables those students' and graduates' institutions to better understand how well their community is doing along the education-to-employment journey.

AfterCollege is another free service that aims "to eliminate unemployment among college students and recent grads by helping students explore jobs and internships based on answers to 3 easy questions: what did you study, where, and when do you graduate."[40] The company provides data on jobs acquired by individuals studying various disciplines at diverse institutions, all with the intention of helping students align their own interests with job and internship opportunities. After-College covers its costs in part by selling advertising space on its site.

Evisors is a fee-based service that connects job seekers to its pool of almost 4,000 advisers, assists job seekers with mock interviews, and provides resume writing guidance and feedback. Bundles of services range from $699 to $1,249.[41] Modern Guild offers a set of services very similar to Evisors, though it sells its services to institutions, which then invite their students to become "members." In this way Modern Guild positions itself as an invitation-only organization, providing a gleam of elitism and exclusivity to its value proposition.[42] Doostang is another fee-based service, with prices ranging from $9.99 for a two-day trial to $15.95 a month for a twelve-month subscription plan that connects job seekers with job openings and alerts them when individuals within their personal networks have connections at companies where they have an interest.[43] The company claims that "1 in 4 recent graduates from the top 30 US universities is on Doostang," highlighting its interest in attracting job seekers from some of the nation's most highly ranked institutions, thus sending a clear signal to its employer collaborators about the quality of talent within its database.

In different ways, each of these firms attempts to bring employer organizations and talented individuals seeking jobs into an online community where they can more efficiently find and connect with one another. These kinds of networking communities have the potential to facilitate the college-to-work transition more effectively than many traditional university career services offices, which in many cases still devote a substantial portion of their energies to providing guidance on resume writing and posting job listings. What distinguishes these startup companies from the typical institutional career services office is their relative focus on helping students and recent graduates align their job searches with their talents and interests, connecting those individuals with employment opportunities in relevant industries, and enabling networking between individuals on these platform in ways that can lead to mentoring relationships and other sorts of connections to promote professional development. Because of their position as intermediaries, these organizations demonstrate a comfort in taking fees from employers and prospective employees alike as well as with the notion of selectively promoting the best prospective employees to the employers showing the greatest interest. While this approach results in a playing field that is something other than level, it does align with the interests of the companies and individuals participating on these platforms, or at least those with the resources to make the necessary investments. This may point to opportunities for greater numbers of colleges and universities to treat their own student talent and employer partners in similar ways, if they are not disquieted by the notion of promoting more aggressively the best talent within their pool of graduates.

NEW MODELS FOR CERTIFYING AND ACCREDITING LEARNING

While coaching companies and career services platforms suggest that there are important and valuable ways of augmenting traditional degree programs and associated institutional services, another category of organization makes the more radical proposition that there is a viable alternative to the college degree: certifying or accrediting nontraditional educational offerings.

The Accredible platform, for example, is designed to assist teachers in identifying and promoting what students learn in their online courses, thereby enabling learners to better position their education and skills in the employment marketplace, particularly in a market where "the world trusts a university degree, but you can get a great education without one."[44] Credly takes a very similar approach, though it targets a wider audience of organizations that might be potentially interested in issuing digital badges, including employers, professional associations, licensing boards, cultural institutions, conference organizations, content providers, youth programs, and colleges and universities.[45]

Degreed takes a different approach to assessing the value of different kinds of learning by awarding a score to each so that, in theory, apples-to-apples comparisons can be made across types of learning—*if* you buy into the values that Degreed assigns to different sorts of learning. According to *Fortune*'s assessment of the Degreed offering, "If you graduate from Harvard with an economics degree, for example, you'll earn 3,787 points. If you complete a programming course at Codecademy, that gives you 13 points. Points are tallied and stored on user profiles on Degreed."[46] Company co-founder David Blake said, "We normalize the data to help make the disparate world of education something that's easily understood by employers and others."[47] The company, founded with angel funding totaling $900,000 (including an investment from Dallas Mavericks owner Mark Cuban), was a participant in the Kaplan EdTech accelerator program.[48]

Credential.me provides a portal to resources that allow individuals to test for credit, undertake internships for credit, earn badges, and more while also partnering with colleges and universities to make these credentialing opportunities available to their students.

The do-it-yourself education movement has enjoyed its fair share of press attention over the last several years, but any momentum the movement might have had has been necessarily slowed by employers' continued and widespread reliance on degrees and the brands of the institutions that provide them as markers of individual graduates' quality, skills, and potential. But for a critical mass of employers, it may well be some time before any alternative form of credentialing becomes truly competitive with, rather than just supplementary to, traditional degrees.

CORPORATE CHALLENGES
AND PROJECT-BASED LEARNING

Another group of companies takes the view that credentials are never going to be as meaningful as a portfolio of professional work, and these firms leverage crowdsourcing approaches to problem solving that can assist employers in evaluating the quality of individuals' work and help job seekers develop their talents further through an alternative type of experiential learning. MindSumo, for instance, provides students who have a valid college or university e-mail address with the opportunity to compete in competitive "challenges" by undertaking projects for companies such as Facebook, IBM, and Zappos.[49] In this way, its platform provides students with the chance to demonstrate the quality of their work and attract the interest of prospective employers. In addition, the site connects users to recent graduates already in the workforce who are available to serve as mentors to students as they navigate their journey from education to employment.

Coursolve also connects individuals with opportunities to solve real-world problems at brand-name companies and invites instructors to position these projects as experiential learning opportunities in the context of their academic courses so that students can develop their skills in a rigorous setting and share the results of their efforts in a public setting that might lead to employment opportunities.[50] Companies can browse a database of course projects and instructors, and students can browse a database of company needs in order to find a match so that these problem-based learning opportunities can be incorporated into the instructors' and students' coursework. In this way, Coursolve connects colleges and universities with learning opportunities within employer organizations. Another company, RadMatter, leans in the opposite direction, positioning itself explicitly as a recruiting platform that enables companies to identify talent through the posting of challenges for which RadMatter members then compete to devise solutions. Rad-Matter invites its members to encourage their schools to promote the participation of fellow students so that the pool of potential talent increases.[51]

While many faculty may already work to incorporate real-world projects with known employer partners into their coursework, platforms such as MindSumo, Coursolve, and RadMatter have the potential to expose students to wider networks of organizations and a potentially more diverse set of real-world projects. Additionally, these online platforms may prove especially useful in the context of online courses and point to new ways of incorporating experiential learning opportunities in that kind of course environment. Ultimately, these kinds of learning opportunities represent more modular and atomized approaches to incorporating experiential learning into the curriculum, whether in the classroom, online, or in a hybrid context. Institutions that are serious about partnering with their students to focus on employability may well elect to incorporate learning opportunities such as these, whether they are developed in-house or not, alongside internships, apprenticeships, co-ops, and other longer-duration, real-world learning experiences.

NEW INTERMEDIARIES SEEK TO IMPROVE RECRUITING INVESTMENTS

Many of the firms mentioned above serve in one way or another to push college-level talent into the job market. There are a wide variety of companies, however, focused squarely on talent recruitment, that view the market from the employer perspective and seek to pull talent into open jobs. These companies focus their value propositions around their capacity to verify learning, provide visualizations and analytic capabilities to assist recruiting employers, and leverage scientific approaches to the identification of talent.

Work America, founded in 2013, is a self-styled "first-of-its-kind social impact business." It connects prospective workers to jobs before enrolling them with a school partner that can provide the appropriate training for those jobs; on completing their studies, the graduates begin their new careers.[52] "No student should enroll in a vocational job program without having a job guarantee," Work America cofounder and CEO Collin Gutman stated. "We get jobs for people before they start a college class."[53] This certainly represents a potentially powerful model for creating a more seamless education-to-employment continuum, and one that very clearly considers employability from day one of the academic experience or even earlier, insofar as Work America starts with an employment opportunity. For the moment, however, it may be somewhat challenging to imagine such a model operating at scale or outside the immediate bounds of vocational job opportunities, though the potential undoubtedly deserves testing.

Another organization, Workforce IO, represents a more common approach to aiding the recruiting process. It attempts to simplify the recruiting process for entry-level positions by verifying job skills—such as being able to use basic hand tools, identify electrical symbols, read basic blue prints—so that employers have more to judge candidates by than what they can glean from resumes.[54] Users of the Workforce IO platform are awarded badges that can be listed in their individual profiles and that can be augmented by short-form videos which show them actually demonstrating the level of skills they possess.

Career Sushi is another platform that provides both individuals and companies with the opportunity to present themselves visually in order to foster more effective recruitment of talent. Companies pay to post openings and to message individuals on the Career Sushi platform, and job seekers pay monthly or annual fees for a premium service that reportedly provides them with access to "exclusive jobs" while giving them "increased visibility" in the network, among other benefits.[55]

Gild takes a different approach to helping companies recruit top software developer talent. It uses what it terms a "workforce science technology" to read and analyze individuals' social media data and shared work product to assess developer capabilities and foster "truly merit-based" hiring decisions.[56] Employers pay for access to the results of Gild's analysis. Similarly, Pymetrics claims a scientific basis for its platform's capabilities—neuroscience, in this case—and invites users to play games. It then assesses individuals' cognitive and emotional traits to match them with companies where those traits are purportedly more likely to lead to success.[57]

Kalibrr provides the capacity to deploy skills assessments tailored to the requirements of individual employers (based on its own database of job-specific tests) in order to position those employers to better judge the match between prospective employees and current job openings and to more easily manage job applications.[58] Another firm that attempts to assess the quality of the individuals it presents to recruiters is Venture for America, which focuses its efforts on assessing talent for placement in startup organizations. Modeled on Teach For America, Venture for America recruits promising college graduates, awards them fellowships, and places them in startup companies for two years.[59] Prospective Venture for America fellows are assessed based on attributes such as "intelligence," "character," "grit," "founder potential," and "ability to contribute."[60]

LinkedIn has been a major player—perhaps *the* major player—in the recruiting space for a number of years. Recently the firm began to engage more directly with high school students, who are already considering how to effectively traverse the transition from education to employment, through its University Pages service, which allows students as young as fourteen to network with graduates of the colleges and universities they are considering attending in order to learn more about those institutions and the career paths their graduates pursue.[61] LinkedIn has also announced partnerships with Coursera, Udacity, edX, Udemy, Lynda.com, Pearson, and Skillsoft to have online course completion records automatically populated in LinkedIn profiles, thereby moving the company more directly into the realm of verifying and cataloging educational experiences.[62] It has also announced the launch of a new service called the "field of study explorer," which allows users to identify companies that employ individuals with backgrounds in particular disciplines, thereby enabling its users to understand which companies hire people with backgrounds like their own.[63]

As employers look to make their recruiting investments generate a better return, they are asking their college and university partners to assist them by becoming strategic business partners in the recruiting process. Services from companies like Work America, Gild, LinkedIn, and others point to new ways that institutions might forge a tighter integration between their degree offerings and particular career paths or draw on data visualization, data analytics, and social networking to more powerfully collaborate with their employer partners to produce results that benefit students, employers, and their own institutions.

CODING ACADEMIES AND THE FUTURE OF COMPUTER SCIENCE

Another area attracting significant investor interest and entrepreneurial activity is the "coding academy"—training organizations that teach individuals software development languages such as Ruby on Rails. While these organizations sometimes partner with colleges and universities to provide educational opportunities institutions themselves might not otherwise be able to provide, in some cases they appear to represent a potentially compelling competitive threat to computer science and engineering programs at traditional colleges and universities, and some may offer the most realistic alternative route to a high-paying job—at least for the moment. Because software developers are in high demand, there are many companies attempting to nurture the talent of interested individuals to meet employers' demand for skilled labor. In many respects, these companies seem to blur together, though they can be distinguished by their pricing, the duration of their programs, the modality of their instruction, and the degree to which they focus on job placement as a component of their value propositions.

General Assembly is one of best-known and better-funded such companies. It was "established in early 2011 as an innovative community in New York City for entrepreneurs and startup companies" and is "an educational institution that transforms thinkers into creators through education in technology, business and design at nine campuses across four continents," including U.S. locations in Atlanta, Boston, San Francisco, and Seattle, among others, and global locations in cities such as London, Hong Kong, and Sydney.[64] General Assembly courses, ranging from Web development to data science to digital marketing and more, are delivered at company locations and online and are available for individual enrollment at fees ranging from $3,500 for part-time programs to $7,500 for "immersive" offerings and with "enterprise" enrollment options for employers.

San Francisco–based Hack Reactor offers "the CS degree for the 21st century" in the form of a twelve-week program for $17,780.[65] According to cofounder Shawn Drost, 98 percent of Hack Reactor graduates get jobs, with an average salary of $105,000.[66] Similarly, Launch Academy boasts a 96 percent placement rate and 100 percent retention rate for its ten-week software development boot camp, which costs $12,500. It claims that it "sets itself apart from other bootcamp styled programs via its long-term focus on students' successes after graduation from the program. A structured, post graduation support program in the form of in-person office hours and virtual consults ensures emotional and job-specific support during the initial phase of their new jobs."[67] Austin, Texas–based

MakerSquare, which offers programs in Austin and San Francisco for $13,880, highlights its aim to place "100% of our graduates in engineering jobs within three months."[68]

With locations in San Francisco, Chicago, and New York, DEV Bootcamp offers nine-week courses in software development for $12,200, and unlike some of it peers it makes fewer claims about its role in helping its students land jobs, reminding prospective enrollees that while a "majority" of students found employment "within three months" of completing their programs, "it is ultimately up to you to find and land a junior development position."[69] Kaplan acquired the company in the summer of 2014.[70]

The Flat Iron School in New York City distinguishes itself by emphasizing the importance of its classroom instruction model and its focus on skills development that it maintains cannot be taught via online resources—"from working in teams, to becoming part of the developer community."[71] It also offers an interesting tuition incentive: its programs costs $12,000, but graduates of its Ruby on Rails developer program are entitled to a $4,000 refund if they "accept a position through our jobs placement program."

A variety of other pricing models exist in the market for the would-be coder to consider. Lynda.com offers a subscription model—ranging from $25 per month to $375 per year for individuals, with group pricing plans for employers—that provides access to a library of video tutorials in areas such as game design, 3-D drawing, and software development.[72] Code Avengers offers twelve-hour online courses with per-course pricing options ($29–$39 per course) or bundled options, as well as per-student pricing for colleges and universities that want to enroll students in Code Avengers courses.[73] Codeacademy, located in New York City, distinguishes itself by offering free online coding courses, some provided by students themselves.[74] The company bills itself as "rethinking education from the bottom up" because "education is broken."[75]

Although the names can be difficult to distinguish among, and the offerings in the code academy marketplace can difficult to differentiate at first glance, the companies attempting to meet the market demand for skilled coders to take a variety of approaches to program delivery, competitive differentiation, pricing, and more. It is, clearly, a heterogeneous cluster of organizations with different approaches to developing talent. While faculty, deans, and other senior leaders within the computer science and engineering departments of traditional colleges and universities may well cast aspersions—however fairly or reflexively—on the quality and depth of instruction provided to enrollees at these academies, there are undoubtedly useful ideas to be found in the way these companies approach the market for those within the traditional higher education community.

So, while Hack Reactor's twelve-week program may or may not truly represent a twenty-first-century equivalent to the traditional computer science degree, it does appear to be meeting a market need and attracting a high caliber student. Likewise, students weighing the benefits of a four-year, $200,000 computer science degree from a top university against a nine- or twelve-week program for less than $20,000 that may have them earning a six-figure salary within a few months will have to consider their options carefully. And when the potential lost income from four years of schooling is factored into the equation, these coding academies may look even more attractive. Indeed, if colleges and universities don't take the opportunity to consider how they and their students might benefit as a result of partnerships with some of these sorts of organizations or by mimicking and adapting some of their features and services, it is not altogether too far-fetched to speculate that one day some traditional institutions could find themselves replaced by these newer market entrants.

EDUCATION ENTREPRENEURS AND THE THREAT OF SUBSTITUTES

While it may well be an overstatement to suggest, as Codeacademy does, that education is broken, there is a growing willingness on the part of many constituencies to consider a wide variety of educational alternatives and substitutes. Witness the widespread mania that greeted MOOCs when they burst on the scene in 2012, not least from legislators who saw in them a way to potentially reduce college cost as well as, perhaps, state education appropriations. A few years later MOOCs don't look all that different from garden-variety online courses, which have been around for more than two decades. But MOOCs have brought a different crowd into the conversation, and they, as one strand in the evolving history of online learning, may yet help point to new ways of conceiving of learning. Two recent initiatives that have the potential to represent meaningful substitutes for traditional models of higher education—Udacity's collaboration with AT&T to deliver nanodegrees and the Minerva Project's global hybrid bachelor's program—share some important features with the companies described above: they look at different ways of packaging educational experiences, they consider different pricing models, and they tailor their delivery models to the audiences they are attempting to serve.

In the late spring of 2014, AT&T and Udacity announced a partnership to develop and deliver credentials, of a sort, that are composed of a series of online courses taking less than a year to complete at a cost of $200 per month.[76] Udacity's vice president of Business Development and Partnerships, Clarissa Shen, calls these nanodegrees "credentials built and recognized by industry with clear pathways to jobs." They are "compact, flexible, and job-focused credentials that are stackable throughout your career."[77] In addition to making a $1.5 million investment in the project through its AT&T Aspire arm, AT&T will be making "up to 100 paid internships available to top students who complete nanodegrees."[78]

If this sounds a lot like corporate training, that's not surprising. After launching in 2012 as one of the first MOOC platforms, Udacity famously transitioned little more than a year later to focus directly on the corporate training market. What distinguishes Udacity from the myriad corporate training providers that have been in the marketplace for decades is that it brings a sheen of rigorous academic bona fides to its efforts, by virtue of its roots in Stanford University, and explicitly sets out to develop an alternative form of degree offering—one that can deliver value by virtue of the scalability of the MOOC model, thus potentially generating revenue growth for its investors via low-price offerings delivered at scale.

Taking a very different tack is the Minerva Project, founded by former Snapfish CEO Ben Nelson, who secured $25 million in venture funding with an eye toward creating an "elite" online undergraduate liberal arts institution. Apart from striving to be elite—presumably a proxy for quality—Minerva is otherwise interested in breaking the mold, particularly insofar as "all the teaching will take place in intensive, interactive seminars, many conducted online using Minerva's specialized videoconferencing system."[79] Yet, the plan for Minerva calls for students to still cohabitate and study together in a cohort model, traveling around the world together in the course of their studies, living for a semester at a time in San Francisco, Buenos Aires, Berlin, Hong Kong, London, New York, and Mumbai—locations Nelson cites as "the greatest cities on the planet." Annual tuition for Minerva is $10,000, though one can expect living expenses to be significant.[80] Minerva is aiming to keep total annual costs below $30,000.[81] After receiving applications from almost 2,500 prospective students, Minerva accepted 69 and yielded 33 enrolled students who formed its initial cohort in the fall of 2014.[82] In order for its program to achieve accreditation, Minerva affiliated with the Keck Graduate Institute in the summer of 2013 under the name Minerva Schools at KGI.[83]

Neither Udacity nor the Minerva Schools at KGI leave the entirety of the traditional model of higher education behind, but they have incorporated new approaches and features not unlike those found in many of the startup companies seeking to deliver new forms of value in the higher education and employability marketplaces. Udacity and AT&T have joined forces to design a relevant curriculum in ways analogous to Rensselaer and IBM's collaboration around cognitive computing, but Udacity and AT&T have also focused on compressing the time to degree while lowering costs and marking out a pathway to specific employment opportunities. Minerva represents a potentially powerful new way of combining online curriculum with place-based, cohort-driven learning opportunities on a global scale, though as yet the school's plans have not explicitly called out a focus on employability. For an institution that will certainly have to earn its pedigree, a focus on employability may well become a necessity before this first cohort of students completes its program.

DRAWING LESSONS FROM THE EARLY ENTRANTS

The institutional initiatives, legislative efforts, and entrepreneurial ventures described here are for the most part in quite early stages, and it will take some time before these approaches to employability and work readiness reach a point of maturity—assuming that some, if not all, of them eventually do. For the time being, then, they represent interesting provocations, suggestions, and opportunities rather than best practices or proven methods for establishing a more seamless pathway from education to employment. Some may even turn out to be game changers. Taken as a whole, these initiatives suggest a number of ways in which colleges and universities, in collaboration with their industry, government, and nonprofit partners, might think about integrating study and work in deeper ways in order to better prepare students for the world of work and to create new opportunities for employer partners to participate in that preparation.

The more compelling features in the work of these institutions and companies include, but are not limited to, accelerating learners' time to market by accelerating their time to degree; demonstrating a compelling return on investment vis-à-vis the price of a given educational or training program; connecting learners to mentors in their fields of choice; reporting on placement rates in ways that make the return on investment more transparent for students and parents; developing industry-relevant curriculum in partnership with key employers; drawing on data science to inform various stakeholders about the productivity of their career services; and serving as a strategic business partner to employer recruiters.

Given the growing number of institutions experimenting with employability solutions, the increasing value of venture investments in the education sector, and the rapidly expanding set of companies seeking to provide work readiness solutions of their own, few institutions can afford to stand still when it comes to helping their students and recent graduates navigate the transition from education to employment. Those institutions that do decide to engage more deeply in this work will have many decisions to make, and the choices will not always be simple or clear. In many instances the choices may force them to reexamine their assumptions about their purpose, mission, and values. The stakes are significant, so it will be best for institutions to consider their options and approaches with care and, wherever possible, to base those decisions on good evidence, existing models, and the capacity to adapt and tailor those models to their individual needs.

3

DESIGNING THE FUTURE THE
GEORGIA TECH WAY

Situated in Atlanta, the Georgia Institute of Technology is a public university with research expenditures totaling over $730 million.[1] It hosts more than 14,500 undergraduate students and 6,900 graduate students, with large numbers of students enrolled in its engineering, computer science, and business programs. Ranked among the country's top five engineering institutions for undergraduates by *U.S. News & World Report*, Georgia Tech's visibility and reputation has been rising steadily both nationally and internationally in recent years. The institution's leadership remains very ambitious and is seeking to place Georgia Tech "among the most highly respected technology-focused learning institutions in the world."[2] An important component of the institution's reputation is its relationships with industry and the many firms that seek to recruit its graduates.

"We're public, so we have a different mission from many universities," Steve McLaughlin, the chair of the School of Electrical and Computer Engineering at Georgia Tech, told me.

"We've always been a very industry-facing place. That's in our DNA, and it differentiates us. One of our primary missions is economic development, so job creation is a real part of our mission. We are inundated with companies seeking to hire our students."[3]

Georgia Tech's Professional Education unit is an academic division within the university that has especially close relationships with industry, delivering online and hybrid master's programs and for-credit online summer courses for undergraduates, as well as courses, professional certificates, and other noncredit offerings targeting working professionals, transitioning veterans, and other nontraditional students. Approximately 95 percent of the division's revenue comes from its corporate customers, said Nelson Baker, the dean of Professional Education at Georgia Tech and an associate professor in the university's School of Civil and Environmental Engineering.[4] Baker is very much a believer that students, employers, and institutions alike can benefit from a shared focus on employability, and, most importantly, by maintaining competency for individuals throughout their careers. He sees growing evidence that research universities like Georgia Tech can make a meaningful contribution in this area. "Companies are more adept at picking the universities that can give them what they need," Baker told me. "There's also increased activity in the form of companies going to the state legislature to put pressure on public institutions like ours to address talent needs."[5]

In response to such pressure, in early 2014 Georgia governor Nathan Deal announced the creation of the High Demand Career Initiative, which will "bring together the heads of Economic Development, the University System of Georgia, our technical colleges and schools, along with key leaders in some of our important private-sector industries" in order to "hear directly from the employers of our state about what they expect their future needs will be," as well as to give "our institutions of education the chance to get ahead of the curve in preparing tomorrow's workforce."[6]

For Georgia Tech, the focus on employability is not only consistent with its identity; it is a big reason why its graduates are in such high demand. The university extends special efforts to assist its students in gaining exposure to a wide variety of real-world professional experiences. Given the university's focus on these matters, the leadership at Georgia Tech understands that partnerships with employers will continue to play a key role in the ongoing evolution of the institution, as its most recent long-term strategic planning effort demonstrates.

PLANNING FOR 2035

After arriving at Georgia Tech in 2009, President G. P. "Bud" Peterson set in motion a strategic planning process that invited the university community to imagine what the higher education landscape would look like at the institution's 150th anniversary in 2035. The result of that effort, "Designing the Future: A Strategic Vision and Plan," was released in the summer of 2010.

"For the strategic plan, we looked out twenty-five years and we saw three scenarios in higher education—two extreme and one in the middle," Leo Mark, the associate dean for Academic Programs and Student Affairs for Professional Education, told me. "At one extreme, nothing changes. At the other extreme, we envisioned a scenario where people go to college for only one or two years and where they enter the workforce on two-to-three-year contracts, with the hiring company having no long-term obligation to them. We imagined that these students would come back six to seven times throughout their career for more education. And when people go through eight or nine jobs in a lifetime and have no corporate benefits, for an institution like ours, it's really a matter of attending to the needs of the adult learner."[7]

While such a model for the integration of study and work would represent a significant transformation of the general model that exists today, it may already be taking shape in the minds of some, including among students around the world, as the Zogby Analytics survey undertaken in collaboration with Laureate Education showed. As those poll results illustrated, university administrators aren't the only ones imagining a future higher education experience characterized by a lifelong, on-demand learning model.

The Georgia Tech one sees today, then, is an institution preparing for a number of different possible futures, including one where the structure of education offerings and the model for the delivery of those offerings will need to be designed to serve a different kind of journey for a different kind of student. Ultimately, that journey may well look much less like a linear path from the domain of education to the domain of employment and much more like the "learn-certify-deploy, learn-certify-deploy" model described by Christian Terwiesch of the Wharton School.[8]

In the context of a higher education environment where the dominant employability pathway is expected to move from education to work and back again, the role of employer partnerships is naturally key to the future of Georgia Tech's work. Indeed, just as external partnerships of various sorts play a key role in Georgia Tech's identity today, the university's strategic plan envisions a future in which they remain very much central, where "strategic alliances with universities, companies, institutions, and governmental and nongovernmental organizations that align with our mission" will be integral to the institution's effort to "bring the world to Georgia Tech."[9]

One area where those partners can have an impact is in helping Georgia Tech reimagine the design and development of curriculum. Certainly the university's leadership understands that the traditional formats for the design and delivery of education programs, as well as the methods used to assess student progress, will need to continue to adapt to the changing needs of their students and their corporate partners. "We anticipate developing flexible and individualized degree programs to prepare students for careers that are unimaginable today," the authors of the strategic plan write. "These will require ingenuity in balancing disciplinary depth and interdisciplinary breadth as we make it easier for students to take advantage of expanded opportunities for elective courses, minors, multiple degrees, and carefully designed, customized curricula. Student progress will be organized by new design elements and evaluated by criteria that are more flexible and relevant than standard tests and grading schemes, fifteen-week schedules, and credit hours."[10]

Georgia Tech has long been recognized not only for the quality of its academic offerings but also for its co-op program and focus on cocurricular learning opportunities. The university's strategic plan demonstrates an understanding of the important role such experiences play in developing the talent of students and preparing them for the world of work. "Much of what students learn is gleaned outside of the classroom, and this is also important in preparing them for success after graduation," the plan states. "Georgia Tech has a rich and strong history of providing the student support services and co-curricular learning opportunities that help our diverse student community acquire and apply life-learning skills."[11] In particular, the plan points to the value of "competitions, short courses, co-curricular activities, and workshops aimed at fostering a culture of innovation and encouraging student creativity and entrepreneurship."

In addition to preparing for a future where curriculum, assessment, and cocurricular activities must continue to adapt, and where industry alliances will play an important role in bringing the world to Georgia Tech, the university leadership is unambiguously ambitious with respect to bringing Georgia Tech to the world and it sees an important role for partnerships in that context as well. "Georgia Tech's reach and impact in 2035 will extend beyond the physical dimensions of a presence in Atlanta and Georgia, as our 'campus' extends to a global network of partnerships."[12]

Additionally, like other institutions that have seen the power of online and hybrid learning, as well as the market impact of more recent experiments with MOOC's, to extend their reach globally, Georgia Tech sees its reputation for technological innovation as creating a special point of leverage in its preparations for the future: "Boundaries of time, distance, and culture will shrink as Georgia Tech contributes to educational applications of the virtual world, using electronic technologies and future media to engage and support our students, faculty, staff, and alumni throughout their lives."[13] In this way, not only is the Georgia Tech of today preparing for a very different higher education environment in 2035, but it is also preparing for the development of a very different Georgia Tech. As the institution approaches its 150th anniversary, the strategic plan's authors write, "the technological research university of the future must be innovative, continually recreating its educational experience and its research programs to produce the kinds of talent and discoveries that the future will require."[14]

FROM MISSION TO VALUE PROPOSITION

"I've been visiting schools with my college-bound son recently," Doug Williams, the senior associate chair for the School of Electrical and Computer Engineering, told me, "and they're all bragging about their relationships with corporations because of the current focus on jobs."[15] For some institutions, attention to corporate relationships, work readiness, and employability is a relatively new thing. In certain cases, these institutions are simultaneously seeking to expand and deepen their employer partnerships just as they set out to persuade parents and prospective students that the degrees they offer will lead to good jobs. By contrast, Georgia Tech is working from a position of relative strength, with long-standing, deep relationships with industry, government, nongovernmental organizations, and other employing bodies. But even an institution like Georgia Tech sees opportunities to integrate the realms of study and work in more profound ways to the benefit of students, faculty, employers, and other stakeholders.

"We've had well-known companies come and ask, 'Why aren't your students talking with us?'" Williams said. "And companies realize they have to become more engaged in order to have more visibility on campus and get students more interested in talking to their recruiters. I've seen a lot of companies in a last few years asking, 'What can we do to better engage and recruit here?'"[16]

In order to understand how Georgia Tech is answering that question for its corporate partners, I went to see Greg King, the director of strategic partnerships at the Georgia Tech Enterprise Innovation Institute, the university's principal outreach organization for the business community, who explained: "Corporate relationships with universities can take many forms, but generally they involve one or more aspect of recruitment, philanthropy, research, economic development, or a business/vendor relationship. From the university element of economic development we are seeing a continuum of involvement with the university in acquiring top talent, then developing that talent via professional and executive education."[17] In other words, the multiple dimensions of these relationships are beginning to be approached in a more coordinated and intentional fashion, both by the organizations seeking deeper relationships with Georgia Tech and by the university itself. For example, the institution's Capstone Design Expo, which provides students with the opportunity to collaborate in small teams to tackle a variety of technological and industrial challenges, is a case in point. Companies can sponsor the competition or propose projects and sponsor specific teams, and not only do they benefit from the students' creative responses to these challenges, they also have an opportunity to develop working relationships with students that may ultimately lead to their being recruited into their organizations.

Once they see the power of building these sorts of relationships with students, companies want to engage with students and faculty in other ways as well, including providing suggestions for improvements to curriculum. The university's willingness to take these suggestions, however, is naturally limited, and partnerships with industry will inevitably raise important boundary questions.

As Zvi Galil, the dean of College of Computing, explained to me, "It's kind of challenging if one company comes to us and says, 'We want x.' But that may be too company specific, and the university cannot do this."[18] Williams amplified the point:

"When companies give input on undergraduate curriculum, I have to hear it multiple times, not just once. They're more free with advice at the undergraduate level, maybe because it's more structured."[19] While the university seeks to be responsive, Williams, like Galil, noted that there are times when it might be necessary to consider carefully where to place the line between being responsive and putting the institution's independence and reputation at risk. "I read recently that Grumman is building a dorm for the University of Maryland for a master's program," Williams added, referring to the Northrop Grumman partnership with Maryland's flagship institution for a program in cyber security. "That's an interesting boundary question."[20]

Charles Isbell, the senior associate dean in the College of Computing, was even more pointed on this matter: "Even at Georgia Tech, where you have this notion of being directly connected to work, there's a tension between the short-term needs of companies and the mission of the university to provide something more robust for the long-term. Every year some company comes to us with a whole new idea about our curriculum that would force us to change everything we do, and we don't do that. Then in three years they come back with a completely different idea about the curriculum. The two sides are always going to be pushing back against one another. Universities have the responsibility to push back."[21]

If employers are prepared to respect the rights of faculty to be the final arbiters with respect to when and how the curriculum should evolve, there are many opportunities for important forms of mutual engagement, and co-ops provide an exemplary case for this. At Georgia Tech, as at other cooperative education institutions, co-ops are paid professional experiences, typically about a semester in length, that allow students to put the skills they have developed in the classroom and the laboratory to work in a real-world setting over three separate occasions in the course of their undergraduate studies. As King noted, "Here at Georgia Tech we have an excellent experiential education program. Our co-op program is one of the largest in the U.S. and is over one hundred years old. Companies love it because it allows talented students to work with them and in many ways allows the student and company to sort of interview each other. Students with co-op and internship experiences are also in high demand. Many times the companies they work for will offer them a position after graduation."[22]

One of the biggest obstacles to successful employer engagement on campus, King observed, is that students aren't always as aware of the wide variety of companies and the opportunities they present: "There are some exciting companies out there doing very interesting work, but it may not always be apparent to the students. A lot of the work is in making the companies known to the students, because students don't know them as well as you might think. For the company, being involved on campus through experiential education, student competitions, information sessions, working with classes, and providing insight and feedback in the classroom—all of those things are very important. One thing that we've seen is that when students have a positive experience, they tell their friends, and that really is one of the best ways for a company to share their opportunities and build brand awareness on campus."[23] To attract top students, companies need to be known on campus, and the best way to achieve that is by being involved on as many fronts as possible—something the university has been successful at helping its industry partners achieve. The College of Computing, for example, has a corporate affiliates program with dozens of companies contributing annual sponsorship fees of approximately $20,000 to support programs and, in turn, to benefit from the access to faculty and students these kinds of partnerships make possible.[24]

As successful as these efforts have been at Georgia Tech, university leaders are very much focused on seeing what more they can accomplish, and one area of significant interest—particularly in light of the scenarios envisioned in the strategic planning process—is alumni. "We want to deliver education for life," Baker said. "We're exploring how to serve alumni more effectively."[25] He points to the university's recently launched Online Masters of Science in Computer Science (OMS CS), in partnership with Udacity and AT&T, as one example. But above and beyond serving alumni, Baker and his Professional Education division are fundamentally interested in innovation writ large.

"I see three kinds of innovation," said Baker. "There's pedagogical innovation and the content side of things, so that we can be online at scale. There are new business models so that we can deliver add-ons like tutoring and advising services. And there's credentialing, as with competency-based certifications."[26] He points to the university's recently discussed X Degree Program, which allows students to design their own interdisciplinary concentrations under the supervision of a faculty member: "The X Degree isn't just a content model innovation. It's potentially a business model innovation and credential model innovation, too."

Flexible formats, interdisciplinary approaches to curriculum design, and experiential learning are all critical components of the value proposition at Georgia Tech. At the core of these, however, is a focus on developing a set of life skills—Drownproofing 2.0, or the ability to create one's own job.[27] "Our goal is graduating students who know how to do new things," Williams said. "We don't train them to do one thing but a series of things throughout their careers."[28] For Isbell, the spirit of drownproofing remains an important part of the culture at Georgia Tech, one that is consistent with the objective of equipping students to tackle some of the world's most important challenges. "Drownproofing teaches you how much you can accomplish when you've been pushed," he said, "and we focus on experiences that push our students."[29]

THE DESIGN EXPO

The Capstone Design Expo illustrates one way in which Georgia Tech involves industry expertise to impact the undergraduate experience. The Design Expo has provided seniors from diverse academic programs with the opportunity to collaborate in the design, development, and prototyping of an application for a real-world, interdisciplinary challenge posed by an industry partner, a member of the faculty, or the students themselves. Past event sponsors have included companies such as CAT, AT&T, John Deere, Kimberly-Clark, and Autodesk. Expo sponsors, which may number between one and two dozen in any given year, provide $8,000 each in funding, the majority of which goes to underwriting the program, with small budgets set aside for project teams' product development efforts.

With hundreds of students participating, project teams are typically composed of four to six individuals. Over the arc of their projects, teams will attend lectures by industry leaders and faculty members on a diverse range of pertinent issues related to design and prototyping, including "patenting, industrial design, manufacturing, market research and marketing, business funding, structure, governances, and ethics."[30] In the spring, students present the results of their work at the Expo, where they can pitch their solutions to a panel of judges comprised of industry experts and Georgia Tech faculty.

The university is currently adapting the program, Isbell explained, as it continues to fine-tune the value proposition for what has already been a very successful initiative. "We're moving away from calling it a 'capstone,'" Isbell said, "and we're moving away from a focus on the senior year to a focus on the junior year. It's now becoming a two-semester experience, which provides students with opportunities to interact with more companies and to connect that experience with two courses in design and technical writing that are tied in directly to their projects."[31]

In this way, the program benefits all participants. "Students get obvious benefits," said Isbell. "Companies get work product and recruiting opportunities. And Georgia Tech gets deeper relationships with its partners."[32] Williams noted that there can be opportunities and challenges associated with taking on industry-sponsored challenges, as opposed to faculty- or student-proposed projects: "The ones with industry sponsorship are attractive. There may not be a lot of money, but there may be some equipment available to use, and access to experts and mentoring opportunities. At the same time, the sponsored projects may be pushed on the students a bit harder, and that can potentially cause problems if the students are not as interested in some of those projects."[33] Most students, he reported, work on unsponsored projects, and the key is to get the match making right and connect teams to high-quality projects. In the end, the payoff for students has been significant, particularly as the Expo has grown in scale. "Students used to do presentations in class. Now they do them in public with an audience of a few thousand watching, and that raises the bar."[34]

The participating companies benefit as well, of course, not only by getting real-world challenges addressed in productive ways, but from the branding opportunity to raise awareness among students about their business objectives and career opportunities, as well as by working directly with students to more closely observe their potential. McLaughlin called the Design Expo "the best way to engage companies" because of the contact companies get with students, adding, "I'm astounded at the desire of these companies to get very close to the students and to handpick talent."[35]

VETERANS TRANSITION PROGRAMS

Two other Georgia Tech programs that place experiential learning at the core of their offerings address a niche, nontraditional audience: veterans. The university's Veterans Education and Training Transition (VET[2]) program and its partnership with Workforce Opportunity Services (WOS) and Hewlett Packard (HP) both assist veterans in transitioning from military service to civilian career opportunities. VET[2] is a four-week experience that mixes classroom with workplace learning and functions as a kind of bridge program, teaching veterans how to position the skills they've developed through their military experience to effectively pursue civilian job opportunities. Importantly, when serving niche audiences, it is critical to involve deep subject matter experts who understand the aspirations and concerns of those audiences. In the case of VET[2], the program director is James Wilburn, who served for twenty-two years in the U.S. Army, retiring as a lieutenant colonel.[36]

VET[2] is offered at no cost to qualified veterans, and it links participants to paid internship opportunities that constitute "a four-week-long interview."[37] Veterans spend the first week of the program in the classroom at Georgia Tech's Savannah campus, adjacent to the Hunter Army Airfield, "learning about the differences between military and civilian organizations using customized content provided by the employer."[38] Instruction is delivered by fellow veterans. During each of the remaining three weeks of the program, participants spend forty hours per week in the internship at the employer site and two hours in the classroom. VET[2] is designed to provide veterans with a tailored curriculum and experiential learning opportunity with a prospective employer as well as the opportunity gain input from the employer partner on matters as diverse as performance on the job, resume writing, and effectively positioning oneself to prospective employers. On completion of the program, participants receive a certificate from Georgia Tech.

While the VET[2] operates at small scale today, with just a handful of students, Georgia Tech is committed to exploring opportunities to expand the program and others like it. The university's partnership with WOS and HP to deliver a certificate in IT consulting for veterans transitioning into the workforce demonstrates the potential to deliver programs like this at scale. Announced in the fall of 2013, the WOS program set out to combine Georgia Tech instruction with opportunities for full-time employment at HP on completion of the certificate program. HP underwrites the costs of the program, providing scholarships and laptops to participating veterans. The program focuses on areas such as "development, IT security, cyber security and project management."[39] The initial cohort had fourteen participants selected from almost a hundred applicants.[40]

"WOS approached us because they had a contract with HP in Atlanta," Mark said, "and HP suggested to WOS that they partner with Georgia Tech. HP has now signed up to put cohorts of fifteen to twenty students through a rigorous three-semester program. Georgia Tech is responsible for the academic piece, but the curriculum is informed by WOS and HP."[41] During the first semester, participants study in the evenings. During the second semester, participants spend half their time working at WOS and half their time working at HP. During the third semester, participants work fully inside HP while taking evening classes. Throughout the thirty-nine-week program, participants are employees of WOS. On completion of the program, participants are hired by HP or remain employees of WOS. According to Mark, HP's goal is to create an employment pipeline of veterans trained in IT and project management. He notes that Georgia Tech is currently working with WOS on a number of other initiatives as well.

THE ONLINE MASTER OF SCIENCE IN COMPUTER SCIENCE

Announced in the spring of 2013, Georgia Tech's partnership with MOOC platform provider Udacity and project sponsor AT&T to deliver an online master's program in computer science drew widespread national media attention, covered by the likes of the *New York Times, Wall Street Journal, Forbes*, and *Huffington Post*. Riding in the wake of the massive open online course movement, which had been driven over the preceding year by organizations like Udacity, Coursera, and edX, the Georgia Tech initiative was massively ambitious—the university set a target of reaching ten thousand students with its new program—and was online, but it was neither open nor a course.[42] Instead, Georgia Tech announced that it would offer a high-quality master's degree on a selective enrollment basis, thus establishing a new way for the university to serve the graduate student market along the way.

A number of these features of the OMS CS caught the attention of the media, which was still struggling at the time to make sense of the MOOC hype that it had played no small part in creating. But there was another aspect of the initiative that drew widespread attention: its low price tag, which was reported to be in the area of $6,600.[43] With the OMS CS, Georgia Tech set out to do something big that would draw significant attention and position itself as a leader, and in these respects it succeeded. Aside from the hype, however, there were more practical ambitions to bring more affordable educational offerings to market. "There was already public pressure to reduce the cost of tuition," Baker said. "This is a way to test what can be done in that price range, though pricing could go up."[44]

Enrollment for the program's first cohort took place over three weeks in October of 2013, with the university receiving more than 2,300 applications—85 percent of which were domestic, the exact opposite of Georgia Tech on-campus master's program in computer science. "Where were these students before?" Baker and his colleagues wondered.[45] If nothing else, these figures provided senior leaders on campus involved in the program with confidence that the online program would not cannibalize on-campus enrollments. Ultimately, the university admitted 410 students to the program, with 382 enrolling for its launch in January of 2014 and 20 students deferring their start dates.[46] In the summer of 2014, Georgia Tech anticipated 1,400 fall enrollments, with approximately 250 students deferring their enrollment until spring 2015, at which point the university leaders expected to have more than 2,000 students enrolled.[47] Once the program has 2,500–3,000 students enrolled, it is expected to be financially viable.[48]

The OMS CS audience is, not surprisingly, working adults, with the majority of students being U.S. residents and male.

"We have some PhDs in the program seeking new skills," Baker said. "We wanted a better gender mix, but it's a young field, so there may still be a relatively small pool of prospective students among women between the ages of thirty and forty."[49] Although AT&T is a sponsor of the program, providing $2 million in funding to help subsidize its launch, AT&T employees account for only about 20 percent of the initial cohort of students, though the company should find some of the program's non-AT&T graduates to be attractive prospective hires in a few years' time.[50]

Although students in the initial cohort were averaging 1.5 course enrollments, they soon found it harder and more time consuming than expected, Baker reported. At the start, Georgia Tech wouldn't allow students to take more than two courses at a time. "They were mad at us," Isbell said, "but now they realize they should only take one [course] because it is harder than they expected."[51] Isbell also noted that the university is currently working to figure out how to deliver good academic advising to online students at scale. "Their questions are at the level of the degree program," he said, "not the course level," and this requires a different approach from the university that Isbell considers a priority in advance of the fall 2014 cohort's start. There have also been some garden variety technological challenges for some students as they seek to move seamlessly from the course delivery platform by Udacity to other ancillary tools, such as the course communication platform by Piazza, though problems such as this should be easy enough to address in the near future.[52]

Another area where the initial vision may not sync perfectly with the practical realities of the current program is price, particularly given the time demands of taking more than one course at a time. Currently, pricing is set on a semester basis, with a $301 charge per semester for technology and support and on a per-course basis, at $134 per credit hour, or $402 per course.[53] Taking one course at a time, the program could take four to six years to complete, and thus tuition could ultimately land somewhere around $8,000 rather than the widely cited figure of $6,600 (though an $8,000 master's degree in computer science is still a remarkably attractive offering from such a highly respected institution). As the time to degree completion threatens to extend, however, there is also a potential risk around student persistence, Baker observed, and this is something the university will continue to monitor as the first cohort moves further into the program.[54]

In response to early lessons such as these, the program's leaders are considering a variety of ways in which the program might be accelerated or augmented in new ways. Currently, Isbell explained, there are three options with the OMS CS: taking the program with courses only, taking the program with courses and adding a thesis, or opting for a project that represents three course equivalents, which reduces the program's twelve courses to nine.[55] "We're also considering group projects," he added, "which can save students time and which are also good both for the students and the companies they undertake the projects for. But the projects would have to be evaluated by faculty, so that impacts scalability. So, potentially, it could be something we offer at premium pricing, and we could even insist on a two-week summer residency and have them present their project on campus, and charge an extra fee for that."

While lessons are undoubtedly still be learned, the early performance metrics look positive, and one day the program may even achieve the scale envisioned at the outset. But for the moment, the returns are encouraging enough, as far as the university is concerned. As Isbell put it, there are three kinds of meaningful impact that can already be observed: "There is a reputational impact. Our on-campus master's in computer science applications are up 30 percent. There's an academic impact. This shows leadership, and the students don't look worse than those on campus. And there's an industry impact. There are companies that want to take advantage of this, too, and they want to talk to us about how they can partner with us and help to shape it going forward."[56] Ultimately, the OMS CS could accomplish something much more important than drawing media attention; it could offer new ways for Georgia Tech to deepen its relationships with its industry partners while extending the university's reach both nationally and internationally.

OTHER INITIATIVES

The Design Expo, veteran transition programs, and the OMS CS represent interesting models for bringing industry into the classroom and learning into the workplace. But they are by no means the only innovative integrated study and work programs at Georgia Tech targeting undergraduate students, niche student populations, or graduate or professional students.

The X Degree Program points to not only new content models but also, potentially, to new business models and credentialing models. Still under development, the X Degree is being designed to serve students who are interested in pursuing a more interdisciplinary curriculum that can be shaped to fit their particular needs and interests. "If a student interning with a company identified an area they really want to explore but which might not be evident in their major," King said, "they could work with their adviser to design a set of additional coursework that creates an area of specialty around certain electives while allowing the student to still meet their degree requirements. These programs present an interesting opportunity for a student. As they work more closely with companies, these experiences can inform the directions their studies may take."[57] For example, if a chemical engineering major has an internship or co-op experience that demonstrates the benefits of possessing an interdisciplinary expertise across both chemical and mechanical engineering, then a student might elect to work with her faculty advisers to organize a curriculum focused on that intersection, which, in turn, should better prepare her for her next co-op, particularly if she pursues an opportunity that explicitly calls for the same kind of interdisciplinary skills. The program is also notable insofar as it provides students with a kind of agency in the design of their studies that is consistent with the life skill that McLaughlin indicated as being at the core what Georgia Tech attempts to develop in its students: the capacity to create their own jobs.

Another area of exploration with respect to undergraduates is the future development of bridge program–like offerings not unlike winter or summer term courses in resume writing or interviewing skills but in a fashion that will be more integrated with academic and experiential learning opportunities and that will be delivered in parallel with the traditional semester rather than between semesters, which can potentially have a more significant impact on students' work readiness. Isbell calls these "mini-mesters," and they can be designed to deliver "short, compact experiences for students that are academic and also connect them to companies. There are a whole slew of things we want to teach that we can't give academic credit for. We can overlay these mini-mesters for four to five weeks over our seventeen-week semesters. We hope to have this implemented in the next two years."[58] The mini-mester has the potential to integrate study and work in some interesting new ways by leveraging the programs and relationships the university already delivers. "Being able to start from a clean slate and integrate it with the semester means it can connect with the direction Georgia Tech is already taking with companies," Isbell said. "This can be integrated with our curriculum and complement co-ops, and faculty will be able to be more creative in terms of how they let students learn things—everything from how to interview to how to build portfolios of work."

The Professional Education division's focus on nontraditional audiences allows them to serve a variety of market niches, including international audiences, which can often provide opportunities to develop programs specifically tailored to the needs of particular companies. Mark described a number of new initiatives he is involved with concerning programs in the Middle East in areas such as information security, sustainable electrical energy, and global information systems, with organizations as diverse as Saudi Aramco or the Harris Corporation in the UAE.[59] While such programs may involve a degree of customization to meet the professional development needs of particular organizations, they also provide the university with opportunities to craft market-responsive training solutions that may have broad application to global industry and that can subsequently be evolved to suit other delivery models, such as wholly online or hybrid programs. In this way, such projects assist in keeping the university's curriculum and program formats cutting edge.

Likewise, the OMS CS experience has already suggested to Georgia Tech's leaders multiple ways in which the university might further explore the potential for delivering lower-cost credentials at scale through online delivery, including new opportunities to evolve the packaging and tailoring of curriculum. Recently, for example, the university launched a noncredit version of the OMS CS, which could one day open up an opportunity for the university to also offer a credit-by-exam option. Isbell pointed to the potential for greater customization resulting from initiatives such as these. "Once we have twenty-five to forty courses developed, then we can mix and match material at a more tailored level. Companies want business classes in it too, for example. This allows us to be quicker to market and can help us build partnerships overseas—lightweight partnerships that allow us to modularize education and weave it together in new ways."[60] Operating in the context of on-campus or on-site degree programs, Isbell said, it was generally too expensive to create such specialized bundles. But the move to a noncredit, online offering makes this kind of modularity achievable.

Baker added that Georgia Tech is currently looking at another degree to be delivered online at scale and may even seek to develop its own platform to deliver such programs in the future, while also working with new corporate sponsors. "We currently have two master's degrees with the backing of corporations up and running, and others coming, but the companies don't always want the visibility," he said. "It's a competitive advantage they want to protect."[61] Future projects in areas such as this may not only allow the university to leverage its recent experiences with moving to scale quickly, but they could also allow Georgia Tech to preserve more control over the student experience and retain more of the revenue for itself, resources that could be used to fund additional new initiatives.

EDUCATORS AND EMPLOYERS ACTIVELY STEPPING INTO ONE ANOTHER'S WORLDS

In various ways and to differing degrees, programs such as the Design Expo, veterans transition programs, OMS CS, and other Georgia Tech initiatives echo many of the themes high-lighted in the university's strategic plan and also anticipate the evolving demands for higher education some decades ahead in 2035. For example, each of these initiatives leverages alliances in powerful ways to integrate study and work, some on a global scale. Many of them focus on experiential learning opportuni-ties—whether in the form of design competitions that hone the entrepreneurial spirit or in the guise of workforce development program for veterans—and often these involve the development of real-world work product on behalf of partner organizations that have a stake in the outputs. A number of these efforts re-quire nontraditional approaches to curriculum design and de-livery, with a concerted focus on problem-based learning and significant input from industry partners. Many of these initia-tives create opportunities for interdisciplinary study that align more closely with the needs of the contemporary workplace. Some of these programs have opened up opportunities for new kinds of student outcomes assessment, including the potential for competency-based approaches. Programs like the OMS CS illustrate the potential for new business models that can diver-sify and deepen the way Georgia Tech works with industry. In one way or another, each of these initiatives is about fostering work readiness or strengthening the capabilities of workers al-ready in the field who need to add new skills to advance their careers or tackle new industry challenges.

In combination, these program offerings illustrate how a research university like Georgia Tech can make job creation a central part of its mission. By bringing its substantial resources to bear in fulfilling that mission, Georgia Tech, like other re-search universities, is in a privileged position to assist learners by establishing a more seamless path from education to em-ployment and back again. Of course, the fact that Georgia Tech is succeeding in fostering employability and promoting work readiness, its success to date and its potential for further success in the future, is in large measure a consequence of the ambition highlighted in its strategic plan: namely, to continually re-create the educational experience it offers, as necessary, to produce the kind of talent the future will require.

4

NYU AND THE GLOBAL UNIVERSITY

New York University is a private research university with a global reach, featuring campuses in New York City, Abu Dhabi, and Shanghai and eleven Global Academic Centers located in Africa, Europe, North America, and Oceania, with research expenditures totaling more than $458 million in 2012.[1] The university anticipates opening additional Global Academic Centers—or "study away" sites, as President John Sexton calls them—in South America and South Asia in the near future.[2] The university's flagship New York City campus hosts more than 22,600 undergraduate students and nearly 22,000 graduate students. Ranked thirty-second among national universities by *U.S. News & World Report,* and situated among the top fifty in the major global higher education rankings, NYU has transitioned over the last several decades from an urban commuter school to a globally competitive research university with a focus on the liberal arts and professional education and encompassing colleges, schools, and institutes in a variety of disciplines that include the fine arts, business, education, law, medicine, and nursing. In 2013 the university hosted more than 9,300 international students, ranked fourth in the nation by the Institute of International Education.[3] In 2008, NYU affiliated itself with Brooklyn's Polytechnic University, which it subsequently absorbed into NYU as the New York University Polytechnic School of Engineering in 2014.[4]

Writing in 2007, President Sexton noted that where other research universities have always sought to teach the elite, NYU has been different inasmuch as it has, since its founding in 1831, "consciously sought to teach the emerging middle class and merchant class, students who were propelled to our doors by a desire to learn and succeed, who saw education as an opportunity, not a birth-right."[5]

In more recent years, NYU, like so many other institutions, has felt increased pressure to demonstrate a return on investment for its students and their parents. According to Linda Mills, the vice chancellor for Global Programs and University Life, today's students expect more than just a good education: "Students, particularly those in a private university, realize that going to college may be a necessity but it also better damn well be a ticket to a job, especially with the high cost of education."[6] The global character of the contemporary NYU, Mills reasoned, presents a particular kind of value proposition with respect to employability: "We have begun to rethink the global experience—whether students pursue an internship or if they want to travel and can't be pinned down to a job. If I'm working abroad, what does that mean? I think we're helping students in that we're now positioning them for a global market. They will walk out of any of our three campuses with a set of skills and opportunities. They can talk across languages and cultures. There are many multinational corporations that are seeking experts across global lines."[7]

As with Georgia Tech, NYU has a unit devoted to nontraditional students, most of whom study part time. Dennis Di Lorenzo is the dean of NYU's School of Professional Studies (SPS), which is among the largest such units in the country and has one of the most diversified program portfolios, including undergraduate and graduate degrees and a wide variety of noncredit offerings, virtually all with a professional orientation. According to Di Lorenzo, "at SPS students start day one with a career orientation, whether they're undergraduates or graduate students."[8]

Clearly, work readiness and employability are a concern at NYU. But the university is nothing if not diverse, and it is a complex and sprawling operation spanning continents, nations, time zones, languages, cultures, and attitudes. The leadership views it as first and foremost an urban institution and increasingly as a global institution that is bringing a compelling value proposition to a set of world markets by combining a deep commitment to the liberal arts and academic research with a pragmatic and long-standing focus on professional education. But as NYU's reach increases and its audiences become more diverse, these various objectives can at times appear difficult to balance. President Sexton, for example, is the biggest booster of the university's global aspirations. And while he celebrates NYU's historical focus on serving an emerging middle class that saw education as an opportunity to learn and succeed, he sees the university's mission today as focusing more on the learning than the professional outcomes of its graduates. Perhaps because of its history, NYU is very interested in being taken seriously as a top research university and appears keen to avoid association with anything that smacks of vocational education. And yet, within the university's ranks there are many who comfortably embrace the challenge to produce work-ready graduates and do not see this as being at odds with NYU's mission.

IN AND OF THE GLOBAL CITY

President Sexton has written extensively about what he perceives to be the role of NYU in the global higher education landscape. His writing about the mission of a global university is rich with allusions to ancient civilizations and the global crossroads they established and also infused with metaphorical references to more contemporary forms of networked societies and other technologically and economically powered forms of connectedness. As Rachel Aviv noted in her 2013 profile of Sexton in *The New Yorker*, his "vision of the university is both religious—it is a 'fragile sanctuary,' a 'sacred space'—and optimistic about the values of the competitive marketplace."[9]

In his 2010 statement about his vision for a global university such as NYU, Sexton argues that "the architecture of this new version of the university is genuinely global, with (in the case of NYU) a planned physical presence (manifest in both facilities and the human capital of faculty, students, and staff) on six continents and the ability to accommodate seamlessly a flow of personnel and programs among those campuses."[10] Words such as "seamless," "flow," and "connectivity" are found again and again in Sexton's writing about NYU, underscoring his aspirations for a university that can, in some measure, provide an infrastructure for the seamless flow of ideas and learning across continents and cultures en route to fostering a more connected world. "Anchored in three ideally located, comprehensive 'portal campuses' and complemented in fully connected 'study away sites' around the world," Sexton observes, "the NYU system is designed to allow faculty and students to enrich their research and learning by offering participation locally in a set of the world's idea capitals without compromising connectivity to the rest of the university." In its conception, Sexton's notion of NYU as a vehicle for education that delivers experiences across an array of world cities is not far off from Ben Nelson's concept of Minerva. But where Minerva is just setting out on its journey, NYU's global expansion has been under way for some time and is firmly rooted in its urban locations.

Since its inception, in fact, NYU has viewed itself as being in a synecdochical relationship with the urban complexity that is New York City. Sexton sees the global expansion of NYU as being natural by virtue of the fact that New York City itself is a global city: "For NYU, creating a global network university is a natural response. NYU was created to be 'in and of' the City of New York, and it has developed ecosystemically with the City. New York itself has developed into a fully 'glocal' city, at once global and local in character: its citizens come from every country on earth, and activity generated in New York touches every country in the world daily. As New York has evolved, so also NYU has grown from being 'in and of the City' to being 'in and of the world.' The particular incarnation of NYU as a global network university is a product of that growth process."[11]

Although President Sexton speaks of three "portal" or degree-granting campuses almost as equivalents—the campuses in Abu Dhabi and Shanghai each have a few hundred students today and are expected to have a few thousand at capacity—the New York City campus is expected to remain very much the flagship and "the primary home for approximately 80 percent of NYU's faculty and students."[12]

Be that as it may, the portal campuses and study-away sites across six continents do seem to possess the potential to fulfill

Sexton's compelling vision for a global institution capable of forging a network to support flows of intellectual and cultural exchange, student learning and faculty research, and the development of a global model for liberal and professional education. Of course, there have been more than a few critical voices arguing against such a vision, and the critiques have undoubtedly reached Sexton's ears.

One critic, Jim Sleeper, a lecturer in political science at Yale University, took his home institution, as well as NYU, to task in a 2013 opinion piece in the *New York Times* under the headline "Liberal Education in Authoritarian Places," in which he argued that "if you look past their soaring rhetoric, you'll see globe-trotting university presidents and trustees who are defining down their expectations of what a liberal education means, much as corporations do when they look the other way at shoddy labor and environmental practices abroad. The difference, of course, is that a university's mission is to question such arrangements, not to facilitate them."[13]

Sexton has not missed messages like this, clearly, but neither is he overly concerned with the risks highlighted by Sleeper and others about the potential perils of globalization, observing, "Some of the results of globalization are beneficial to all; others detrimental to all; most somewhere in between with benefits created but unevenly allocated. Whatever its results, globalization is part of the reality of our time."[14]

Again and again, Sexton highlights the virtues of global engagement for NYU students and faculty—not only through the university's portal campuses but also through its study-away sites, and not only through the strength of NYU's curriculum but also through its cocurricular learning opportunities. Sexton notes how "students at sites are able to (and sometimes required to) do community service, internships, and homestays.

Thus, students in NYU Accra serve as teaching assistants in local middle schools or participate in delivering health care to Ghanaians as part of a course taught simultaneously in Accra and New York. Students in NYU London and NYU Prague study acting and filmmaking with some of the great theater companies of those cities. And, students enrolled for a semester of study in NYU Shanghai intern at global companies headquartered in Shanghai."[15]

Where Sexton sees virtue in globalizing NYU's vision for the liberal arts, Sleeper and some other critics of the globalized university see the values of liberal education being diminished as a result of the move into far-flung regions such as Abu Dhabi, as with NYU, or Singapore, as with Yale. "At its best," Sleeper argues, "a liberal education imbues future citizen-leaders with the values and skills that are necessary to question, not merely serve, concentrations of power and profit. Universities that abandon this ideal are lending their good names to the decline of liberal education; turning themselves into career-networking centers for a global managerial work force that answers to no republican polity or moral code; and cheapening the value of the diplomas they hand out, at home and abroad."[16]

It is interesting to note how Sleeper's critique of globalization is coupled with a critique of an education model slavishly in service to corporate employers. Regardless of whether or not Sleeper accurately estimates the risk of such an outcome, it would be difficult to characterize Sexton's vision as one that reduces the university's mission to that of a mere career networking center. Sexton himself has critiqued the narrow focus on jobs as the sole measure of an educational outcome:

Higher education policymaking in the United States and increasingly around the globe recently has been driven by narrow, utilitarian arguments, such as: "Exactly what jobs and how many jobs will be created by this program or precisely what will be the pay-off from the research in which we are investing money?" There are times when such questions are appropriate, but overemphasis upon them forces higher education onto a procrustean bed. Tunnel-vision "practicality" and misplaced notions of "accountability" miss the lesson of history. The big ideas—the ones that pave the road of progress—typically spring from pure research and thought for its own sake, when thinkers enter the trackless realm of intellect not knowing where they will be led.[17]

As Trudy Steinfeld, the assistant vice president for Student Affairs and executive director of the Wasserman Center for Career Development at NYU, said, "You want to educate students, but you want to work with industries in meaningful and appropriate ways. We're not a vocational institution."[18] At the same time, Steinfeld understands that being connected with industry is an integral part of the university's work and not an activity in conflict with its educational mission. "We think that way," she said. "We run our career center as a business. We talk about business development, industry expertise. I'm dealing with these corporate entities all the time, and we bring that back to our students and the academic side to say, 'Here are the skills gaps,' to see if we can address those. It is important to know that we are partners. It means we can help students to prepare for the world that's evolving. If we fail to do that, institutions will be losing ground, and it will show in terms of their enrollment."

In a global context, Steinfeld explained, this work of connecting education with employability can be especially critical, insofar as students may not be well prepared to describe how their global education experiences have more effectively prepared them for the world of work. Indeed, at worst, students may position these experiences in ways that make them look like educational tourists rather than work-ready professionals.

"I had an epiphany three years ago," Steinfeld said. "I asked students in a workshop in Paris, 'Tell me how you talk about your experience abroad to employers.' They thought they could do it, but they were telling them that they were learning French and drinking great wine and enjoying the food. So I asked them why that mattered to employers, and no one could give me an answer."[19] Recognizing that NYU's students were at risk of mischaracterizing the educational and professional benefits of their international studies, Steinfeld decided to take action. "On the plane home, I started developing the idea for this thing called 'Telling Your Global Story' in our career center curriculum." The curriculum focuses on helping students identify what they've learned and why it's relevant to their prospective employers—whether it was learned in the classroom or out in the field. "We're thinking of career development as a continuum of experiences. And the university is embracing that. You don't have to have a formal internship. You could be doing service, or participating in a leadership program. Having a global mind-set is the most important thing."

NYU's experiences tackling challenges such as these provide a number of useful lessons for institutions thinking and strategizing about how best to support the employability of their own graduates, whether in the form of undergraduate bridge programs and experiential learning opportunities or graduate programs delivered in online or hybrid formats or social networking platforms to foster peer-to-peer learning and professional networking. Notwithstanding the university leadership's evident discomfort with accusations that globalization or a focus on career development might result in a diminishment of the quality of the institution's educational programs,

NYU remains a university that is committed to thinking in an innovative way about its connections to industry and its obligations to its students to provide not only a great education but also, as Mills put it, a ticket to a job.

INTERNSHIPS, PROFESSIONAL CERTIFICATES, AND BOOT CAMPS

"NYU doesn't look down [its] nose at professional education," Matthew Santirocco said.[20] Santirocco is the senior vice provost for Academic Affairs and a classics professor. He sees liberal arts education not only as an enriching preparation for life but also as an essential precursor to a professional career or further professional education, with NYU students leaning in the direction of the latter. The economic uncertainties following the recent recession have, in his view, only made the NYU value proposition more relevant. "What we do was always relevant," he said, "but more so after 2008."

Bringing that value proposition to the global market, of course, is no small undertaking. "NYU's DNA was always urban and professional," Santirocco noted. "Now we are a global network as well."[21] Global internships, particularly when treated as part of a continuum of learning experiences, represent an important opportunity for NYU students to build and demonstrate the mind-set that Steinfeld highlighted as being a critical educational outcome, and these programs fall under Santirocco's purview. "Internships have always been a hallmark of the NYU experience," Santirocco said. "But for many years students just moved through a series of experiences. What we are trying to do now is to treat these experiences as points along a continuum or trajectory of learning. But this is still not as deep or pervasive as what happens in co-op education settings."

The university's various campuses and study-away sites provide students with geographically specific opportunities to gain exposure to some of the leading lights in their disciplines. Building relationships on so many fronts, however, is time-consuming and intensive work. As Mills explained, there are occasions when the university leverages its existing relationships to establish internship opportunities and other occasions when it turns to local market experts. "In Accra, Ghana, for example," she said, "we have our own set of contacts. In London we hired a company to help us build those bridges. In Sydney we're going to hire a company. In time it will be homegrown. That's how we can do it efficiently. You don't build internships overnight."[22]

According to Santirocco, those experiences need to be meaningful, whether they are developed with an outside partner or not: "In some sites, yes, we go on our own, in others we have partners. In Berlin we may be partnering with an organization for experiential learning and internships. But the experience is not worthy of credit unless there is academic reflection on the fieldwork and assessment associated with it. Making coffee or photocopying? I don't think so. Having a meaningful set of responsibilities and then a thoughtful and reflective course to accompany them is critical, since the internship is part of the academic experience."[23]

In Washington, D.C., for example, the university's newest, and only domestic, study-away site, Santirocco points to the opportunity for an art historian to participate in an internship or other experiential learning occasion in a gallery, museum, or archive. "It will be thematized in that way," he said. "It's already happening in our Metropolitan Studies Program here on 'the Square,' since the program has a requirement for an internship experience, and there is a course that goes along with it, during the internship, as a corequisite."[24]

This sort of parallel experience of study and work, which can be a requirement from accreditors in some professional disciplines such as law, represents one way of thematizing the learning experience, as Santirocco put it, and treating the work experience as part and parcel of the educational experience—that is, as a continuum of that educational experience, as Steinfeld expressed it. But Santirocco and his colleagues at NYU see opportunities for the university to push further in this direction. While there is a recognition of the fact that other models, such as the cooperative education model, are valid, Santirocco's focus is instead on how to strengthen what NYU already offers. "In our Wagner Graduate School of Public Service there is a capstone project—commercially viable work—embedded in the course, creating not just case studies but also new knowledge," he noted. "The co-op educational model, though, is extraordinary, and the internship is a pale shadow of that. But it doesn't need to be if internships are linked to one another, thematized to align with students' majors, and supported by course work."[25]

A long-standing collaboration between the College of Arts and Sciences and the School of Professional Studies highlights another way of linking study to professional preparation. "A decade ago, when I was dean of the College of Arts and Sciences," Santirocco said, "we created a program with SPS called Professional Edge for our traditional undergraduates to earn noncredit professional certificates. For example, a student might study English, earn a certificate in publishing, and then get an internship in the field. We have similar programs in many other fields ranging from digital graphics, to translation"[26] Students participate in SPS noncredit courses, which range in duration anywhere from a weekend to fourteen weeks, with instruction provided by professionals working in the field. "The challenge," Santirocco said, "is that the number of participating students is not that big."

The program is restricted to students with a 3.6 GPA in order to limit the program to high performing students so that they wouldn't be at risk of neglecting their core studies. Santirocco believes that this, alongside competition from other in-house programs, including double majors and multiple minors, helps explain the relatively low enrollment to date. Di Lorenzo, from SPS, agrees, arguing that the program should really target students in the 2.8–3.2 GPA range, as "those are the people who need it."[27]

Another way for SPS to play in the domain of internships is to be a provider of services to other schools' students. "We have a relationship with the University of Dreams," Di Lorenzo said, referring to the for-profit experiential learning company. "They are all about providing the internship experience; and then students come to NYU SPS, and we teach a class while students live in dorms here for a two-to-three-week period."[28] In this way SPS functions as a kind of bridge program service provider, not altogether unlike a Fullbridge or Koru. Di Lorenzo sees opportunities for SPS to serve other transitioning populations as well, such as veterans, who "need a transition program—critical thinking, writing. They have the hard skills but not the soft skills. I have a proposal for an SPS Veterans Transitions program to get them into industry."[29] SPS is also currently developing a transition program for certain nursing programs.

The Business Boot Camp for Liberal Arts Students is another undergraduate initiative that functions as a kind of bridge program that is, in some respects, akin to programs at institutions such as Dartmouth, Middlebury, and Vanderbilt, though at NYU the program is run out of the Wasserman Center for Career Development. The program was started before the recession but has been proven to be perhaps even more valuable since then. One of the ways in which the Wasserman Center strives to stay current with the employment market, Steinfeld explained, is by drawing on the perspectives of individuals on its employer partner advisory board, which meets twice a year, and by hosting a conference for recruiters. "Several years ago we were at a strategy meeting talking about their talent needs," Steinfeld said. "It wasn't just accounting or business. They needed students from all different disciplines thinking about their businesses before the students even think they might want a career in that industry. So we brainstormed this Boot Camp for Liberal Arts Students, and Morgan Stanley has sponsored this. All the other organizations started benefiting too, and twenty organizations are now involved to provide training and instruction and mentoring. It's those types of partnerships and combinations that can be incredibly powerful."[30]

The boot camp kicks off with a two-day program held in January, with other one-day sessions following throughout the year. "We have a large buy-in for this," Steinfeld said. "The program is free, but we ask students for a deposit, and when they show up they get the deposit back. About 150 students go through the program annually, and we have five cohorts a year. We get keynote speakers, enlist industry partners, and we have tracks in areas like marketing, finance, major ad agencies, social media, consumer products. And our employer partners help deliver the training."[31] The frontline participation of partners is key, in Steinfeld's view, not only to providing a quality education experience but also to establishing credibility with students. "Students trust . . . three things: faculty, industry experts, and friends and parents," she said. "If I bring in the head of some business area from EY or TFA or Morgan Stanley, that has more credibility than me making the same statements."

Given the collaboration across colleges, schools, and centers in areas such as internships, professional certificates, and boot camps, I asked Di Lorenzo about future opportunities to support employability and work readiness along these same lines. "At SPS," he said, "we've already integrated with employers, so that's not our goal. Our next step is to create added value to the rest of the university. Professional Edge is one version of that."

But there are other ways for SPS to add value to other communities. One example is a forthcoming summer program called Professional Advantage, which is wholly distinct from the previously discussed Professional Edge offering. Where Professional Edge helps NYU undergraduates add a relevant professional certificate to their bachelor's credentials, Professional Advantage goes a step further by incorporating real professional experiences. Di Lorenzo explained that "Professional Advantage is a cohort-based, three-week summer program that will provide industry and career exposure to students as well as insight into various industries and the job market for entry-level positions in those industries." At launch, the Professional Advantage program will focus on serving liberal arts students from other institutions who are looking for a summer program that can help them build a bridge to a profession. The longer-term vision, Di Lorenzo added, is to bring NYU undergraduates into the program too.

The aim at NYU is to create options and to harness resources and relationships to make the undergraduate liberal arts experience as supportive of employability as possible. That effort involves not only establishing the right programs but also creating the right incentives and targeting the right audiences, as Santirocco and Di Lorenzo noted with respect to the Professional Edge offering. It also means leveraging the perspectives of employer partners directly by involving them in the design and delivery of cocurricular programs. As Santirocco put it, "We have to have a value proposition that employers understand. In terms of our work with employers, we need to build institutional relationships, not just personal ones."[32]

ENTERPRISE LEARNING

This same spirit of close collaboration and deep relationship building with industry inhabits one of the university's newest divisions, its NYU Polytechnic School of Engineering. Bob Ubell, the vice dean for Online Learning, who plays a lead role in the delivery of the school's online graduate programs and enterprise learning activities, emphasized the importance of following industry's lead when it comes to the identification of market needs but also stressed the importance of leaving curricular decisions to the faculty.

Ubell explained, "We have industry colloquia here on our campus or in Washington, D.C., or in California with senior executives from industry, people responsible for running business units."[33] Speaking with business unit heads is critical, according to Ubell, because if you go to HR, they fear that the programs on offer will eat into their budgets. "We had a banking industry colloquium here in New York City not long ago. The attendees were talking about what they see with our programs and with others' programs that don't satisfy their needs. They say, 'It's nice to have analytics and cyber security degrees, but we need people who know all those things—not subspecialists, but a broader view on data science, mobility, security, and so on.' They don't advise on curriculum. They just discuss issues of importance to them."[34]

The colloquia focus on strategic management issues and are typically run by an industry chair who recruits the industry colleagues she wants to hear from, perhaps fifteen to twenty-five in all, and the school hosts the meeting. Relationships play a key role in organizing these meetings, of course. Ubell pointed to a recent meeting on cyber security hosted by a partner from Goldman Sachs who has a relationship with a chair within the school, and also to another case in which a director at IBM has a relationship with a research director at NYU. But these personal relationships are a starting point, and the important thing, as Santirocco said, is to turn these personal relationships into institutional relationships. The school hosts three or four of these industry colloquia a year, in addition to another ten or so webinars a month (one recent webinar attracted more than 160 attendees from IBM alone).[35] "We also collaborate very closely with our colleagues in research here at NYU," Ubell said. "When we identify a company interested in one of our online learning programs, they may also be interested in our research in that same arena."[36] In this way, the relationships grow beyond the personal and become increasingly institutional in character.

Deepening relationships with industry is not only critical to developing market-responsive curriculum, Ubell argued, but is also key for the growth of online graduate programs within the school. While corporate customers account for a small share of overall tuition revenue today—the vast majority of revenue is derived from individual students—he expects corporate revenue to account for half of all revenue within the next three to five years. To get there, colloquia and industry advisory boards will play a key role. "Curriculum that matches corporate objectives is what ultimately sells."[37]

Equally important, however, is having the right online student experience, according to Ubell: "When you go online with one of our engineering master's degrees, you will experience a virtual environment that is the optimum environment that you would find in industry. Our objective is to provide our industry partners with the opportunity for their global employees to have a single language and style of training that is not balkanized by having contracts with local universities in Shanghai or Abu Dhabi or elsewhere. That's one reason why Goldman Sachs chose us: they want a single global perspective, a single global language for all of their employees."[38]

On the matter of corporate customers asking for changes to or providing input on curricula that threatened to cross an important line, Udell said that "most companies do not want us to customize our master's programs for them. Their objective is to give their employees the same foundation as everyone else; they don't want it to be corrupted by their interests. My office has no direct contact with the curriculum development, which happens in the academic departments. We play no role in designing the curriculum. If a company wants case studies, however, that focus on their business, with the approval of the professor teaching that course, if there's no real significant changes in the curriculum objectives, we will happily do that."[39] A more common request, Ubell said, was for corporate clients to have closed cohorts for their own employees, generally for corporate security reasons. "We will do that," he said, "but we don't think that's the best learning experience. We think the best is linking their employees with others."[40]

Ubell's chief concern for the school and its online graduate programs in continuing to enhance their relevance to the market in order to benefit students, employers, and the institution itself was funding: "We need an integrated alliance of government, industry, foundations, and universities to support funding. And that means we need to engage them in everything we do."[41] He pointed to a recent White House event on cyber security attended by some of the nation's leading companies and sponsored in part by the Sloan Foundation as one example. But he also noted that it's important to have a clear value proposition for the organization that is enrolling employee-students in an NYU program: "We have to show them that investments in this program are more cost effective than the $50,000–$60,000 they'll spend recruiting someone. It builds loyalty among students toward their employers."

Ubell's advocacy for collaboration across industries, institutions, governments, and other stakeholders echoes the views expressed by Thomas Kochan, David Finegold, and Paul Osterman in "Who Can Fix the 'Middle Skills' Gap?"[42] Kochan and his coauthors argue that collaborative programs of this type can ameliorate the risks faced by individual organizations in investing in talent development as these investments become shared with other organizations in a given region, thereby providing all participants with a shared interest in developing the local talent pool. But, of course, this is more easily accomplished—if it can be accomplished at all—on a local level than a global level; thus, a challenge for a global institution such as NYU will be to foster these kinds of cooperative arrangements wherever they operate around the world.

GLOBAL LEARNING OPPORTUNITIES

To understand how industry relationships were being leveraged to support the work readiness of NYU graduates on a global level, I spoke with Eitan Zemel, the dean of Business and Engineering at NYU Shanghai and vice dean of Global Programs and Executive Programs at the university's Leonard N. Stern School of Business, and his colleague Erin O'Brien, the associate dean of Global Programs and Executive Programs.

"Global studies at Stern . . . is targeted at very successful people who don't come to Stern to get a job," Zemel said. "They come to us, still, for work-related reasons—to sharpen their sword."[43] Program enrollees are comprised of senior executives from the world's leading companies. The key element of such programs at Stern, in Zemel's view, is the experiential component and the orientation toward project-based learning. "I would say the innovation in our group is the centrality of the project: real-world projects in the course of study. The students come in with a lot of fire power on their own, and they bring their own projects with them."[44] O'Brien amplified the point: "The project is a huge factor. It's a big motivator for them. It's a place for students to integrate the material in an applied way."[45]

While the students enrolled in graduate programs such as these may not be looking for jobs, the benefits of teaching them can ultimately impact all students at Stern. "The main purpose of the global degree programs is to serve as a laboratory for Stern where we can try new things—new content, new uses of technology, new forms of pedagogy, new types of schedules, and so on. We are faced with a certain profile of student," Zemel said, "so we do different things and we can experiment."[46] He pointed to the potential to explore new forms of pedagogy and also highlighted the downstream benefits that accrue to program design and faculty research: "The standard way of teaching is a very comfortable platform. 'I, the professor, know, and you, the student, don't, so let me teach you what I know.' That is not the approach we can take in these programs. Our faculty are experts. They know what's going on in their fields, better than anyone. But our students, collectively, run units with thousands of people, invest billions of dollars. So there is a give and take in class. The experience influences the research that the faculty are doing. It also influences our teaching in other programs. And this is a net benefit to Stern. So we treat this spillover as one of the formal objectives."

Interacting with students such as these has helped shape new interdisciplinary programs, O'Brien added: "Historically, Stern graduates were attracted to jobs in consulting or banking. Now the people in demand, and the skills in demand, are different. There's a tremendous need in the field of business analytics. In response to this we launched an MS in business analytics, which can be described as the intersection of business and technology. There's a need for schools to reorganize their offerings to fit where the skilled workers are needed today."[47]

At SPS, Di Lorenzo's team is building its own kind of professionally oriented master's degrees for a global marketplace, and its approach is consistent with the history and mission of the school. "Everything we do at SPS is with an eye to connecting people to their industry," Di Lorenzo said. "In the early days, SPS was very focused on noncredit, skills-based education, where students needed exposure and skills to move on in their careers, and they did it in a noncredit way. Industries have realized that continuing education is valuable, and they know they need a new kind of leader. That's why we've developed our industry-focused master's programs with a focus on management skills, research, writing, analytical skills. The curriculum is woven together in a very academic way, but also with that skill-building core."[48]

Historically, SPS has focused on serving adult students, often studying part time, who seek education to advance their careers or change careers altogether. But Di Lorenzo said that the focus on career outcomes is becoming more pervasive. "Now we're seeing that students need to think about our kind of programs even in high school or in undergraduate general education programs," he said. "A small example of this is that high school students might be interested in a one-week summer intensive in film, real estate, photography, or sports management."

Commenting on tensions between the academic mission and the professional education mission that plague other institutions, Di Lorenzo said, "The problem that I have with that debate is that it's 'applied skills' versus 'general education.' We need to give the students both. Traditional liberal arts doesn't currently give you both."[49] He pointed to the forthcoming Career Pathways offering as a way of accomplishing both. "I want to do this well and offer it as added value for our traditional students. We can connect our students with industry. That's what this school does."

One of the ways in which Di Lorenzo hopes to further expand the impact of his school's relationships with industry is through the delivery of master's degrees on a global scale via hybrid learning. "We're looking at a global master's degree, a blended approach where we have, say, a university partner in Mumbai. We hire the faculty, and it's our curriculum. We have intensive, local on-ground delivery for the first two weeks of a semester, then maybe the students go to internships with courses delivered by technology during that period, then they come back to the course on-ground for a week or two at the finish. The local partner gives them connection."[50]

Di Lorenzo believes there's a global—or "glocal"—market that needs what NYU offers, and he anticipates hosting cohorts in places like Shanghai, New York, and Paris and possibly involving faculty, who may be recruited from the local pool of alumni, collaborating to connect students studying in these diverse locations. These local faculty also bring relationships with industry to support the identification of internship opportunities. "One question is, do we start in new markets where we have no relationships or existing markets where we do but the opportunity may be smaller?" Di Lorenzo wondered. "The latter case makes career development easier."[51]

He also foresees transnational learning opportunities in certain degree areas, such as SPS's master's degree in tourism, where students might start with two weeks in Paris, study online during an internship, and then finish in London or Abu Dhabi. Di Lorenzo acknowledges that curriculum for programs such as these requires "a loose template to allow for localization," and he anticipates having offerings of this sort available in 2015 once the curriculum is completed.[52]

NY YOU: THE KNOWLEDGE COMMONS

The role of alumni in connecting students to experiential learning and career development opportunities is something that NYU is giving increased attention to on a variety of fronts, and not just in the context of its global master's programs. If, as Steinfeld observed, students put particular trust in industry experts, then alumni possessing that kind of expertise can bring real value to students as coaches and mentors. "We have a large mentoring program with about 1,400 NYU alums, mostly done online."[53] If it were possible to scale that pool of coaches and involve greater numbers of NYU alums in mentoring current NYU students, Steinfeld suggested, the employability benefits could be significant and deep.

This, in fact, is a project that Rick Matasar, vice president for University Enterprise Initiatives, is currently working on: the establishment of what he calls a "peer-to-peer engagement platform that will take the university out of the equation altogether, [thereby] allowing for more innovation."[54] With a beta version launched in the spring of 2014, Matasar refers to the new platform as "NY You: The Knowledge Commons." Ultimately, he hopes to involve as many as 60,000 of NYU's 400,000 alumni on the platform, which will function as a community of alumni, employers, and students augmented by a variety of career services. The platform will be populated with what Matasar referred to as curated content, some of it public domain material, such as MIT's OpenCourseware, and some of it NYU materials. A portion of this content will take the form of lessons, while another portion will feature whole courses or other kinds of packaged offerings. Lessons might be linked to one another to form a kind of curriculum. And in addition to the original NYU content and open educational resources, community members can publish content of their own. "The next Sal Khan could emerge from this community," Matasar suggested.

The platform is designed to support a variety of forms of interaction, signified by three buttons on the platform's homepage: Create, Discover, Request. The Create button allows members of the NYU community—whether students, alumni, faculty, or others—to publish content. The Discover button allows members to view content, study content, share content, and embed content for their own purposes. The Request button allows members to submit requests for teachers to connect them with industry mentors, to seek information and opinions from each other, and to find collaborators for new projects. At all times, a ubiquitous Share function allows members to post the results of projects, connect with career services, and seek job opportunities.

One of the ways in which Matasar envisions members utilizing the platform is their diagnosis of gaps in their skill sets relative to job opportunities they may be interested in pursuing and then drawing on the community to address those gaps. The university has partnered with Noodle, an education services company, to provide a platform for tutoring services. Tutors are drawn from the NYU community and certified by the university but employed by Noodle. If this all sounds a bit like Collegefeed, Evisors, Doostang, MindSumo, Coursolve, and even LinkedIn, among other businesses aiming to help those making the college-to-work transition, that's because it does. What distinguishes NY You from these other platforms, though, is that it's a closed community—though a closed community of potentially great scale with potentially rich links to employment opportunities around the world.

Among the entrepreneurial ventures attempting to provide some of these same services, there are typically two kinds of approaches. Some start from the vantage point of the student or education institution and attempt to push the recent graduate into the employment marketplace. Others start from the vantage point of the employer and attempt to pull the bright talent into their pools to support the recruiting objectives of the employers with which they are aligned.

NY You represents an intriguing effort to establish a community that encompasses both of these approaches at once in a way that leverages the institution's reputation for academic rigor and network of high-quality students and alumni. In doing so, Matasar said, a number of downstream benefits will accrue to the university: "NYU doesn't have a football team to establish community, so this is another means of creating loyalty. Because NYU is 'in and of the city,' the loyalty is often to the city and not NYU."[55] The rate of alumni participation in institutional advancement is below that of NYU's peer institutions, Matasar noted, and one of the potential benefits of establishing something like NY You is to create "a deeper sense of NYU as special via this curated network." If the platform can achieve this objective by creating a space for a broad community to engage in meaningful forms of exchange, and alumni giving rises as a result, then the costs of maintaining the platform are, in Matasar's words, "a rounding error."

Beyond alumni giving, Matasar made the case for other indirect forms of return to the university, among them increased tuition resulting from growing enrollments in part-time programs. "This is also an on ramp for NYU, and particularly for SPS. SPS offers everything from noncredit personal enrichment courses to job-related certificates to degree programs, but we have a small percent of enrollment from our community; this provides us with a way to connect our community to SPS."[56]

Because the NY You platform permits members to establish more narrowly focused professional communities at a college or industry level through its Share function and Request button, the platform also has the potential to serve as a recruiting and matching service in ways not dissimilar to companies such as Gild, Pymetrics, or Kalibrr. It may also offer a "checking service" to provide verification and certification (for a fee) to employers, much as companies like Accredible, Degreed, and others are currently trying to do.

It's a compelling vision—and particularly interesting inasmuch as NYU is seeking to draw on the strength and scale of its own community to provide students with opportunities to respond to challenges, post project results, network with alumni in the industries they hope to work in, and connect with job opportunities at the same time as it aims to support its alums' recruiting efforts, grow university advancement, build loyalty to the NYU brand, and drive tuition growth by promoting the diversity of education offerings delivered by divisions such as SPS. While NYU is not going it entirely alone—Noodle is engaged to provide tutoring and other alliances may be established to strengthen the NY You value proposition—the university is taking on a large portion of the heavy lifting in fostering a new set of services for the members of its community, regardless of where they are on the college-to-work continuum. To the extent that NY You is successful at leveraging the NYU community to these ends, the platform will provide an interesting option for other institutions that might be considering outsourcing arrangements with companies.

WHERE BRAND IS NOT ENOUGH

One of the most significant changes in higher education over recent decades has been the shift to a focus on outcomes, where all stakeholders seek a clearer return on investment, whether they be students, parents, universities, employers, or governments. Furthermore, today, the focus is not just on student learning outcomes but on institutional outcomes as well, as measured by individual students' career success and regional economic development.

"The idea of the university as an intermediary between knowledge building and career preparedness was never intentional," Matasar said. "Universities are really, at the core, about knowledge and fun, and not career readiness, whether at the undergraduate level or nonprofessional graduate level. And that's what they've been optimizing for—hence the climbing walls and concierge services priced for the rich. So the connection to careers has not been explicit." But something has changed, he underscored. "Over the last fifteen years, the percent of the whole of the higher education student body that the rich represent has diminished," he noted, "and employers have also become less tolerant of training the untrained. The upper-middle schools, not the very top ones, have to now focus on outcomes as a result. Where brand is not enough, you have to show outcomes."[57]

But Matasar doesn't see outcomes supplanting brand. And while NYU may not fit the definition of a "very top" school—it depends on where one draws the line, as well as how one ranks institutions—it is still an institution with an enviable set of assets, an expanding global reach, and an increasingly strong reputation. The university's legacy of serving the emerging middle class by providing practical education and professional training can play an important role alongside the institution's strengthening brand. And that may be exactly what the market is seeking: brand and proof of solid outcomes.

"Employers say, 'Don't worry about the technical stuff, just focus on soft skills, teamwork, problem solving, and we can teach the technical stuff,' but they don't mean it," Matasar said. "They still want the 1500 SAT student with great networks. But Joe Blow from Staten Island isn't going to fit that mold, and so he needs an outcomes focus on top of everything else. It's additive."[58] Disruptors, Matasar added, can disaggregate the traditional functions and the contemporary functions of the university—the knowledge piece, the career piece, the fun piece. But what NYU's focus on initiatives as diverse as experiential learning, corporate education, global programs, and social platforms suggests is that another powerful approach is to aggregate these capabilities in a new, forward-looking fashion that links learning, personal enrichment, and professional development.

5

NORTHEASTERN UNIVERSITY AND THE FUTURE OF EXPERIENTIAL LEARNING

Northeastern University is a private research university based in Boston with additional campuses in Charlotte, North Carolina, and Seattle, Washington, and with research expenditures totaling $98 million in 2013.[1] Its flagship Boston campus hosts more than 13,200 undergraduate and 6,800 graduate students. Ranked forty-ninth among national universities by *U.S. News & World Report*, Northeastern recently broke into the top 200 in the World University Rankings at number 184. Founded in 1898 as the Evening Institute for Younger Men at a Boston YMCA, it grew over the next several decades to become one of the nation's largest postsecondary institutions, with almost sixty thousand students in the 1980s. Over the last thirty years the university has transitioned from being a commuter school featuring a large number of part-time enrollees to an up-and-coming research university with a focus on the business, engineering, and health professions, among other technical and professional disciplines.

Northeastern is widely recognized as one of the nation's leading experiential learning and cooperative education institutions, with its students completing almost 8,000 co-ops annually at one or another of the university's nearly 3,000 employer partners around the world; in addition, the university's career services office is ranked second in the nation by the *Princeton Review*.[2] The university is also increasingly recognized for its global character, hosting more than 7,700 international students in 2013 (ranked seventh in the nation, according to the Institute of International Education).[3] More recently, it has organized its geographic expansion activities under the Global Network, which connects its domestic campuses, international co-ops, study abroad programs, global research collaborations, and other international programs and initiatives under a new paradigm of connectedness, interdependence, and mutually reinforcing value propositions. The university also hosts one of the nation's larger continuing and professional education divisions, the College of Professional Studies, which focuses on serving working professionals through an array of on-ground and online part-time programs, particularly at the master's level.

EMPLOYERS SHAPE THE AGENDA

Like NYU, Northeastern is comfortable blending rigorous academic experiences with professional education programs and experiential learning opportunities. In fact, the university leadership views this combination of experiences as being very much what contemporary students require. "Employers shape the agenda today," Northeastern president Joseph Aoun said. "Our focus in higher education is on getting the students what is best for them. We want the students to learn to learn, and we want the students to learn to earn a living. The cost of education is high, and people are making this investment, and they are saying, 'I want this investment to give me what I need.' And what they need is both—education and work preparation."[4]

President Aoun has been a longtime champion of integrating study and work, and he views this as part and parcel of Northeastern's fundamental value proposition: "The purpose of education is educate students for a life of fulfillment and accomplishment, and the way to do that is integrate the classroom experience and the work experience. This is a way to get students to see the world differently, to see opportunities differently, and to see where their passions lie. This is an obligation that we have. This is part of our mission."

Of course, even at a professionally oriented institution such as Northeastern, there are boundary issues when it comes to driving the education agenda. And while Aoun credits employers with shaping the agenda, that does not mean they control it. Despite the university's deep relationships with industry, at Northeastern—much like at Georgia Tech or NYU—it is the job of the university leadership to push for an educational experience well beyond mere vocational training. "It's difficult to prepare students for the workplace because the workplace is subject to change," Aoun noted. "So the job here at Northeastern is to prepare them to be competent, first of all, and to be global. That's how we do it. We want them to be global, through co-op, for example. We don't want them to be comfortable with just one type of industry."

Rather than promoting narrow career objectives among its students, the university's programs, both academic and co-curricular, encourage a diversity of experiences, often global in character. The institution's NUin program allows select students to spend their first semester studying at one of several international sites. Its semester-length study abroad offerings, Dialogue of Civilization summer programs, and international co-ops provide students with a host of international study, service learning, and paid professional work experiences around the globe. In combination, these and other programs every year take thousands of students abroad to study in more than one hundred countries. For Aoun, providing this kind of diversity of experience is critical to helping students discover their passions and preparing them for the diversity of professional experiences that await them after graduation. "There is not one type of employer. Companies that are in a startup mode are very different from companies that are multinationals. Employers who are global are going to want people who are fearless, who are going to jump in and meet their objectives."

That's the kind of fearless student Aoun wants his institution to produce. But as much as he feels Northeastern has done to support this, he still sees an opportunity for the university to do more—particularly at a global level, but at a national level as well. "The integration so far has been between the university campus and the workplace," he said. "But in the same way that you have multinational workplaces, you have multinational universities. In the past, universities expected the workplace to come to their campus. Now what we are doing through our Global Network is that we are going to the learner and we are going to the employers in distant geographies— online and on-site—in India, China, the Philippines, and the United States. If you wait for the workplace to come to you, it no longer will." While the key nodes in the university's Global Network are still domestic, with its campuses in Boston, Charlotte, and Seattle, the vision for its expansion includes both domestic and international sites dedicated to a variety of different types of university activities, from academic programs to research collaborations to co-curricular activities to alumni relations and so on. Central to all of these activities, however, is the university's relationships with its employer partners, wherever they operate around the world. As Aoun says, the task of a professionally oriented global research university is to take education to those employers and those employment markets, wherever they may be.

Technology has already played a supporting role in helping Northeastern serve its growing global audience, and Aoun sees opportunities for emerging technologies such as adaptive learning solutions to further augment these efforts and thereby strengthen the university's value proposition. "We are at the outset of customization and personalization," he said. "You customize a program for an employer and you personalize a program for a learner. I believe the opportunity is to bring the two together. So I see a couple of opportunities. The first is that you cannot expect the employers to come to you; you have to go wherever they are. The second is the intersection of customization and personalization."

It's possible to see these opportunities taking shape in a number of current initiatives under way at Northeastern, ranging from how its leaders approach program design by drawing on employment data and employer perspectives to inform the development of curricula, to how it is working to bring experiential learning to the online student, to how it is attempting to tailor programs to career changers seeking to join high-demand professions.

STRATEGY AND PRODUCT DEVELOPMENT

There is a growing body of literature decrying the corporatization of higher education and the mimicry of business practices by colleges and universities. For some, the very idea that an institution of higher learning would need to engage with consultants to define a strategy or adopt so-called best practices to, say, accelerate product development is simply at odds with the mission of such an institution. For others, the work of identifying a need in the market and defining a differentiated strategy for meeting it in order to compete more effectively against other institutions seeking to meet the same market need is simply practical. Over the last few decades, the influence of consultancies and market research organizations on administrative responses to changing market conditions has become increasingly noticeable, and today it is commonplace for colleges and universities to work not only with advertising firms but also survey organizations and research firms that can help them better understand their target markets and reach their prospective students more effectively while at the same time developing degree, certificate, and noncredit programs that more closely align with the observable needs of the market. More recently, institutions have begun developing some of these capacities in-house, so that university leaders can have more direct control over these market investigations and hold their strategic decisions somewhat closer to the vest.

Northeastern is one such university that has made increasing investments in recent years in the development of an in-house market research capacity to assist in guiding its strategic decision making about which markets to serve and by what means. Sean Gallagher, the university's chief strategy officer, explained how Northeastern's strategy function "really began in 2009, and it remains fairly unique insofar as it's a central function working across disciplines and schools, and also in that it's really about being market focused, understanding trends in the environment, the needs of employers, the competitive landscape, changes in demand, and new market opportunities."[5] The strategy function, which Gallagher oversees, was born out of a crisis, the recession of 2008, and the opportunities it presented. "There was an innovation task force convened in 2008 when the president created a group of senior leaders to begin to brainstorm about new opportunities and moves that could happen during the disruption that was occurring in the environment—and to think about how to be a bit bolder and more innovative while so many colleges and universities were retrenching."

In a moment of great economic uncertainty, the university leadership elected to play to its strengths, and for Northeastern that meant leveraging the relationships that constituted the core of its value proposition and competitive differentiation. "As a university that's focused on global experiential learning and has long been defined or differentiated by its integration with the world of work and its attention to employers," Gallagher remarked, "that put the university in a unique position to create a function—or a set of resources or new initiatives—that was going to seek to harvest the potential of all these employer connections." Over the past five years those intentions have taken shape in the university's expansion into new geographic markets, most visibly in its Charlotte and Seattle campuses, but also through "the routinization and expansion of market research and program feasibility studies" to drive growth decisions. The decisions to enter markets such as Charlotte and Seattle were the result of systematic analyses encompassing the assessment of dozens of prospective markets and involving the input of hundreds of area employers.

Of course, inputs such as these drove not only decisions about which markets appeared most attractive but also decisions about which programs to bring to each market. "The last five years have seen tremendous growth in academic programs,"

Gallagher said. "Countless master's degrees, undergraduate minors, and so on have been launched for a variety of reasons: the increasing focus on things that are global, new faculty that have been brought in that are leveraging their expertise in applied research in various fields, significant thinking about what are the fields of the future and what are the degrees that could be interdisciplinary, like sustainable building systems and biotechnology professional science master's degrees, health-care informatics, information security, video game design—those types of fields." In the early phases of that growth there was less of an expectation that evidence would be provided to justify the launch of new programs, but that has changed, Gallagher said, to the point where it is now a routine process across the university as colleges and schools consider bringing new offerings to market.

> That's something that's been developed and codified in the university's new program approval process. Not only is there the typical cursory look at peers and competitors and job market demand, we do actual interviews and deep job-market analysis, very rich competitor scanning, and we look at all sorts of data and trend information to not only inform whether a given academic program should be a go or a no go but to tell us what the program should look like, what sorts of competencies and skills it should address, what kind of graduates it will create, what the opportunities for them will be and what students might be looking for. We do that through student research, as well, focus groups, surveys, and things like that.

In addition to conducting surveys and reviewing trend data, Gallagher and his team put feet on the street to gather input firsthand from their current and prospective employer partners.

The way that we grew domestically, being so focused on employers, was pretty unique, and that's part of the ethos here. Often we talk about having two primary customers, if you will: the students, as is the case at all universities, but also the employers. In addition to the diverse methodologies and inputs we tapped into or designed to assess where might there be a geographic market where we could meet a need—everything from surveying, direct interviews, regulatory reviews, search engine analysis, competitor scanning, things like that—what was very unique was getting on the ground as we studied markets and meeting with employers about what their needs were.

The payoffs from such labor-intensive research efforts can be both significant and diverse. Gallagher outlined how mutually reinforcing forms of value could be derived from such efforts. "Our interests were not only in enrolling working professional students but in creating a talent pipeline for the employers, in being able to send co-op students to these new regions, and also in some cases doing research with these companies. So this expansion would allow us to better integrate with the employer environment and better serve that employer environment—employers that are national and global," including organizations like Bank of America, Duke Energy, and Siemens.

For Gallagher, the benefits of this kind of work increase as the university examines greater numbers of potential markets. "We talk about a vision for a new type of research university where its economic impact and integration with the world and the world of work and employers is not place bound, [where] it's not largely related to our economic impact in Boston and the employers that are in the Boston area." To the contrary, Gallagher believes that the university's programs are being made stronger by virtue of their having been tested in a variety of markets by increasingly diverse sets of employers. "By taking our master's in computer science to Seattle," he claimed, "the program is now much more informed by the experiences of the Seattle startup environment and Amazon and Microsoft and some of the technology titans out there." In this way, the research function Gallagher has assembled supports and strengthens the institution's academic mission by providing a valuable set of inputs to curriculum design and continuous improvement.

What strikes Gallagher and the corporate organizations he's talked to is that practices such as these aren't more widespread. "We have consistently heard from employers in these conversations—and I think this is part of the reason why employers have been so engaged with us—that, typically, universities have never left their Ivory Tower and come to meet with them before. They're amazed that universities, and especially research universities or top-ranked universities, aren't having that dialogue and aren't being proactive." For its part, Northeastern is very proactive, according to Gallagher. "In Seattle, we met with two-hundred-plus employers, and we've done that in other markets as well. We wanted to shape our offering for Seattle in response to the employer interest and employer partnerships, in addition to what the student interest might be or what we could see with more passive looks at the marketplace." The net result to date, in Gallagher's view, has been a stronger alignment with the employment markets in Boston, Charlotte, Seattle, and elsewhere. But he still sees an opportunity for the strategy and research function to achieve more. "We talk a lot about alignment with industry, programs that are industry aligned," he said. "But I think the ultimate goal is not just alignment but much more of an integration."

The design and development of the university's master's degree in Regulatory Affairs for Drugs, Biologics, and Medical

Devices, offered through the College of Professional Studies, represents one example of how the institution takes a place-based approach to tailoring programs to meet the needs of high-growth industries through dialogue with employers and the identification of the competencies demanded by those employers. As John LaBrie, the dean of the College of Professional Studies and vice president for Professional Education said, "Boston has one of the most robust biomedical industry sectors in the United States, and the genesis of the Regulatory Affairs program came out of a need in that particular sector for individuals who could essentially take medical devices and drug development and move them through the regulatory process. That involves everything from understanding how to measure and conduct drug trials in the marketplace to moving a particular drug or medical device through the regulatory process."[6]

To better understand that need, the program's designers convened a meeting of area industry leaders. "We brought a summit of individuals in that sector to the table in the early stages, and we really started developing a strategy that ultimately resulted in the graduate degree program. It was largely industry informed and industry led, along with the collaboration of the college, which had an interest in growing a graduate degree program that was unique to the university and which no other school within the university was delivering at the time." That summit, LaBrie said, focused on understanding, in a detailed way, the capabilities industry required in this area: "The degree program really was developed largely by the list of competencies that those biotech companies needed to take to their fundamental research around drug discovery and move it through a regulatory environment."

While the initial investigation regarding the opportunity for a master's degree in Regulatory Affairs began by localizing the design to the needs of the Boston-area market, the program ultimately proved attractive to other markets as well, including some international markets. "Even though it has a localized mission at the front end," LaBrie said, "it was found to be very attractive on a national and international level, including India and Brazil. So it ultimately attracted a much broader audience beyond Boston." As Gallagher suggested, each opportunity to port a program to a new market creates a learning opportunity that can further strengthen that program—both at the core, where its constituent elements remain constant, and at the margins, where it may be tailored to the needs of a particular geography or regulatory environment. "That process really is much of what we're talking about when we talk about working with the corporate community to develop meaningful credentials for a workplace environment," added LaBrie. "Much of higher education has been almost antagonistic to the corporate community, and if you sit and listen to what they're saying, much of what they're saying can be largely informed by a very sophisticated intellectual activity that merits a graduate degree."

ONLINE EXPERIENTIAL LEARNING

As an institution associated with cooperative education, one of the top priorities at Northeastern is to build experiential learning opportunities into as many programs as possible. As the university's expanding portfolio of online and hybrid degree programs has grown, it has become increasingly important to look for ways to incorporate experiential learning into these programs. A couple of recent initiatives suggest how this distinguishing feature of the Northeastern experience can be integrated into these newer modes of learning.

As President Aoun explained, experiential learning at Northeastern is, in many respects, "about integrating the co-op experience back into the research experience"—that is, the students' academic studies. "Before they go off [on the co-op], they are doing research, and when they come back they are doing research. This way they learn not only by thinking but by testing. That's the most important part. You are testing yourself. The students learn what they are good at, what they are not good at. They learn also about teamwork. They learn in an environment they are not familiar with. They get out of their comfort zone."

For a university serving thousands of students online (some in fully-online programs, others in hybrid programs) predominantly at the master's level, with programs often delivered through the College of Professional Studies and with most of the students already working, the challenge of creating this integrated professional and academic experience requires new approaches. As LaBrie underscored, "The very premise of the graduate degree programs that we work in and the population that we target in the College of Professional Studies is that we exist to assist our students in advancing their careers and their livelihoods. Unlike a liberal arts education that's working at the undergraduate education level to give people a well-rounded education for the rest of their lives, many of our students are coming to us based on the notion that they want to advance their careers. So it's imperative for us to really take seriously the notion that our degree programs will map to the career choices of our students."

To serve career advancers or career changers effectively, LaBrie argued, understanding the outcomes the employment community seeks is key to ensuring that employer are "getting the talent pipeline that they want and they deserve," and experiential learning opportunities can help ensure the development of the capabilities employers require. "Our success model is largely built on the employability of our students. If our students are heading out to the workforce ill prepared to survive their next career move, then we're failing them." But developing significant experiential learning opportunities for online students requires an approach different in some respects from the traditional co-op model. "I think experiential learning—broadly defined as an opportunity for students to do meaningful, hands-on activities where they get to apply the theories and concepts they've learned in the classroom and to be allowed a period of reflection so they can draw out the learning that happens within that context—will become increasingly critical to all of higher education," LaBrie observed. And that includes online learning.

In 2013, the College of Professional Studies conducted a small pilot in an online, master's-level course that served as an elective for a variety of degree programs focused on project management, leadership, and nonprofit management. The objective of the pilot was to provide fewer than a dozen students with an opportunity to design and implement real-world projects within their employer organizations that addressed a strategic priority but which sat outside their current realms of responsibility—undertaking a kind of mini co-op. As Ellen Stoddard, director of Cooperative Education in the College of Professional Studies, said, "This is not 'try and buy.' This is a custom co-op for someone who's already employed."[7] Students enrolled in the online course spent the first several weeks identifying a suitable project and a project sponsor inside their organizations who was not currently supervising them.

According to LaBrie, the pilot constituted an attempt "to replicate the cooperative education model that has all of the principal tenets of experiential learning and that would articulate it in such a way that it would allow a working adult studying in an online environment to have the same type of learning outcomes that we traditionally have seen in a co-op program." While a project conducted in the context of a single course taken part time is certainly different from a traditional co-op (which at Northeastern is typically a six-month paid professional work experience), it can present many of the same kinds of practice-based learning opportunities that, when coupled with reflection, can constitute a powerful integration of study and work. Admittedly limited in scope relative to the traditional co-op, online experiential learning projects of this sort can also provide benefits that other co-ops typically cannot.

"I think the added benefit of the co-op-at-work model over the long haul may in fact be our ability to engineer an intelligence stream that hardwires both the university and employer community in such a way that our faculty and students and the employer will symbiotically be learning the same things out of this process," LaBrie suggested. "The student employees really become the conduit to that transfer of information back and forth, making the university a much more robust place that understands immediately when the market is shifting by virtue of what our students are telling us in real time through these projects." In this way, experiential learning integrated with coursework functions as a kind of real-time laboratory for curriculum refinement as well as a continuous opportunity for strategic data gathering on evolving market demands and job-specific competency requirements. Optimally, this kind of activity at scale would reduce the time cycles in program revisions and allow faculty to shift curricular strategies in a more timely fashion in ways that sync with current market needs, and that, LaBrie speculated, ultimately can create a stronger value proposition and competitive advantage for the university and for the college.

As Stoddard noted, a pilot such as this points to the potential for driving greater enrollment growth as employers see how curriculum can be aligned with their business objectives in effective ways. Additionally, the kind of collaboration among faculty, students, and employers required of courses such as this present opportunities for deepening employer relations in other meaningful ways, whether by identifying opportunities for employers to inform the design of curriculum in related programs, by establishing opportunities for greater numbers of traditional co-ops inside the employer organization, or by positioning projects as a kind of capstone that amounts to "an integrated demonstration of competency," among other things. The payoff can take many forms, but the overall objective is to permit employers to guide course and program designers and faculty and administrators in promoting work readiness.

In Northeastern's College of Social Sciences and Humanities, another kind of online experiential learning initiative has recently been launched by Rebecca Riccio, director of the College's Social Impact Lab. In the summer of 2013 and the spring of 2014, Riccio delivered a MOOC entitled Giving with Purpose, a free, open-enrollment, noncredit, online course designed to teach the fundamentals of effective philanthropy. It was delivered in collaboration with the Learning by Giving Foundation and hosted on the MOOC platform edX, and it is currently the only MOOC offered by the university. The course provided participating students with the opportunity to nominate nonprofit organizations to receive grants from funds provided by the Learning by Giving Foundation as well as the chance to take an active role in evaluating prospective grant recipients and then distributing $100,000–$150,000 dollars in grant funding at the conclusion of each course cycle.[8] As with many MOOCs, Giving with Purpose drew thousands of students and in so doing constituted a special opportunity to deliver a compelling online experiential learning opportunity at scale. The university is currently exploring opportunities to integrate the MOOC with degree program offerings so that interested students can further advance their philanthropy education.

As these projects suggest, there is great potential for incorporating meaningful experiential learning opportunities into online courses and programs, whether they be for credit or not for credit and whether the courses serve a handful of students or thousands. As online and hybrid programs become increasingly commonplace, particularly at the master's level, and particularly for an audience of working adults, incorporating these kinds of potentially powerful experiential learning opportunities will be critical to the future of the learn-certify-deploy economy.

Another recent initiative at Northeastern tackles online experiential learning in the context of a new set of master's degree programs that function as a kind of bridge offering for the career changer or recent college graduate looking to top up his skills to improve his work readiness as he pursues career opportunities in high-demand industries. The university's ALIGN (Accelerated Link to Industry through Northeastern's Global Network) programs are designed to help college graduates with a strong foundation in quantitative analysis jump career paths by combining a handful of bridge courses with master's-level academic programming (delivered in a hybrid format) as well as paid work experience in a professional field related to the curriculum.[9] The programs promote employment opportunities in high-demand fields such as bioinformatics, computer science, energy systems, and information assurance by providing tailored master's programs that enable students to effectively augment their current competencies and capabilities with additional skills that will enhance their employability. Students can enroll in these hybrid programs at any of Northeastern's three campuses, in Boston, Charlotte, or Seattle, and will participate in at least one full-time co-op in the course of their studies at one of the university's employer partners.

In some respects, the ALIGN program is analogous to the business-focused bridge programs offered to current or recent undergraduates at Dartmouth, Middlebury, Vanderbilt, or elsewhere. But in other respects ALIGN is significantly different in that it equips its graduates with a master's degree while also assisting them in strengthening their resume by providing opportunities for full-time paid co-ops. Of course, paid professional experiences also offer the added benefit of helping to offset program costs. After piloting a program in computer science in 2013 for the Seattle market, the university set out to offer eight distinct master's programs across its geographies in the fall of 2014. While the model looks promising, it will be some time before the university has results to point to that can demonstrate its impact.

INTEGRATING EXPERIENCE AND LEARNING

Northeastern has in recent years been an institution in transition, evolving over the space of a few decades from a high-enrollment commuter school to a highly selective research university. What has been consistent throughout that transformation is the university's focus on aligning study with professional experience and drawing on its close relations with the employer community to continuously inform the strengthening of its programs and value proposition. As President Aoun and others observed, a university focused on education and employability must prepare its students for an employment market that is constantly shifting. The task of the university, then, is not to prepare laborers for specific jobs, but to nurture work-ready graduates who are prepared to succeed in an economy where jobs will come and go and where new and previously unanticipated professional categories will emerge. The Northeastern experiential learning model represents a special case for reconceiving how academic study, rigorous scientific research, and cocurricular work experiences can aid in the development of a talent pool. It also presents a special case for imagining how a geographically distributed institution—a network—can function to nurture local talent pools tailored to the needs of particular, regionally specific industry clusters, whether in computer science, health science, environmental science, or other high-demand fields.

What these university leaders make clear, however, is how much potential there is to unlock with respect to fostering employability and work readiness—not only at Northeastern, NYU, Georgia Tech, Southern New Hampshire, or Western Governors but across the landscape of higher education. I asked LaBrie where he saw the greatest potential for Northeastern to advance its efforts related to work readiness, and he highlighted the potential for greater collaboration with employers in the area of assessment to inform the continuous improvement of curriculum. "One of the things that Northeastern has understood anecdotally is that co-op has informed our curriculum over time. I think the silver bullet here for us, and the one thing that I would find tremendously exciting, is if we could figure out systematically how to draw on the data that's being gathered by our co-op students and our students engaged in other forms of experiential learning to hardwire that into a system where we can, in real time, analytically identify work trends or shifts in the marketplace from an employer perspective." Having that kind of data in hand, he suggested, would strengthen the university's ability to respond to changing market needs from an academic perspective. Additionally, data of that kind would enable a new kind of cutting-edge research on pedagogy and open up the potential for identifying new kinds of credentialing models that are tied more closely to competency.

Gallagher agreed.

The next innovation that comes to mind for me is an open marketplace in terms of the credentialing system; in other words, more fluidity with respect to the skills and knowledge and competencies that are acquired in the workplace from an employer and what's acquired in higher education. We can already see that there are startup companies and technologies and different pilots and initiatives and new types of institutions like Western Governors University. We can see what Southern New Hampshire University is doing. We see shifts in policy like the direct assessment approval by the U.S. Department of Education for competency-based education. These things are beginning, but I don't yet have a good sense of what the uptake will be in the employer environment, which is still very reliant on traditional degree credentials.

As these cases suggest, today's college and university leaders are very much at the beginning of a shift toward a more concerted focus on employability and work readiness; most initiatives are new and rapidly evolving. Few have extensive sets of evidence they can point to in order to demonstrate their impact. But they do constitute a healthy variety of collaborative experiments being undertaken by institutions and employers that can not only permit them to more actively step into one another's worlds but also, in so doing, design a more efficient and effective continuum of education and professional development experiences. Of course, the plane of experimentation is not infinite, and there are boundaries that must be considered. Collaboration between universities and employers will always hold promise, but it will also necessarily come freighted with certain tensions. Higher education may never be prepared to function in a truly market-driven way, not least because it is a regulation-driven market. And thus employers' collaborations with colleges and universities will be complicated by this asymmetry, even as they work to identify and maintain ever more common ground and shared interests.

"At the intersection of higher education and employment, there's a tremendous amount of overlap and redundancy and inefficiency," Gallagher observed. "If you believe in the idea that it's a marketplace, you would think that there would be some market solutions to this. But higher education is a highly regulated domain, and the single biggest provider is the government, or public institutions." While Gallagher expressed optimism about the potential for further innovation in the realm of employability, he said that the regulatory structures of higher education may have to be more thoroughly reconsidered in order for more expansive and truly market-driven innovation to take hold. "You have these structures that are codified throughout higher education," he concluded, "from the federal financial aid system to the charters and missions and governance policies of public and private universities to accrediting bodies and professional associations. And it's complicated. I think there are tremendous and interwoven structural barriers to change. Some of those structures may need to adapt or be re-envisioned in a wholesale way to actually open up a market where you could have more efficiency and more value created."

Gallagher's observations about higher education regulation, governance, and financing functioning, whether intentionally or not, as barriers to more radical forms of innovation are well taken, and these are undoubtedly matters worthy of further consideration by policy makers and regulators in the years ahead. At the same time, however, it would be a mistake to underestimate how much opportunity remains for college and university leaders and their employer partners to strengthen the focus on work readiness within the regulatory, governance, and financing structures that currently predominate. Northeastern's focus on market-tested product development processes and work in the realm of online experiential learning underscore just how much can be accomplished within the context of these structures. The important opportunity is for more institutions to begin to engage with their current and prospective employer partners in similar ways. In doing so, these institutions will contribute in important ways to helping higher education leaders prepare to explore what the next generation of integrating study and work might look like in the decades ahead.

6

BEING DIFFERENT

When I began teaching twenty-five years ago, I never heard anyone refer to students as "customers." Today, it's commonplace, just as it's routine to hear institutions in neighboring areas referred to as one another's "competitors," presumably because they are thought to be vying for the same customers. Over the last several decades, growing numbers of university leaders have come to recognize all too well the increasingly diverse pressures to be more relevant and market responsive—pressure from governments, from parents, from students, from employers, from boards of trustees.

One way of demonstrating relevance is through differentiation: offering something different from one's competitors or offering something similar to one's competitors but in a different way and with different points of emphasis. These days, most college and university leaders are not coy about being competitive or about needing to compete effectively aided by a differentiated value proposition. And when the word on so many lips is "jobs," it's not surprising that growing numbers of higher education institutions seek to build a differentiated value proposition around the Drownproofing 2.0 imperative:

providing their graduates with the skills to obtain, or even create, their own jobs.

I began this book by asking what colleges and universities should be doing differently to assist their students in preparing for the world of work. One way to frame the answer to that question, as Mona Mourshed and her colleagues at the McKinsey Center for Government did, is to suggest that employers and university leaders need to actively and purposefully step into one another's worlds in order to strengthen the alignment between what education providers deliver and what employers expect and need. University leaders as diverse as Drexel's John Fry, SUNY's Nancy Zimpher, Clark's David Angel, and Plymouth's Wendy Purcell agree that new kinds of relationships with employers are required to effectively produce what Purcell pointedly refers to as the "graduate plus."

Virtually all institutions can claim relationships with employers, of course, so this is by no means a novel concept. But these kinds of relationships, whatever their current character and focus, can still be more academically and professional substantial, can still be more aligned, and can still move beyond alignment itself toward a real integrated effort at supporting employability and improving the prospects of a match between recent graduates' skills and capabilities and the requirements and demands of the contemporary workplace, as Northeastern's Sean Gallagher and numerous others I interviewed suggested.

While newer entrants to the education marketplace, like Udacity and Minerva, may be attempting to forge breakthrough models for the delivery of higher education and may yet prove to have useful things to teach us about integrating study and work in deeper ways, institutions like Georgia Tech,

NYU, and Northeastern, among others, show how it's possible to innovate around issues such as employability on the basis of their traditional and long-standing strengths.

Thus, when the president of the United States or a state governor or state legislators or other stakeholders advocate for a focus on job preparation at our colleges and universities, it isn't necessary to view this challenge as constituting a Faustian bargain for the higher education community. It should, however, be viewed as a call to action—a collective call to action in which we can all participate by shaping a response, just as many of the institutions and companies highlighted here are working to do. Institutions as diverse as Southern New Hampshire University, Middlebury College, and Harvard Business School are striving to equip students with new skills and capabilities that will increase their value in the job market. At the same time, companies like Koru, Collegefeed, Coursolve, Work America, and Hack Reactor are pointing the way toward more entrepreneurial solutions to the challenges presented by the education-to-employment transition. And these organizations may have much to teach the higher education community as well, whether by virtue of their interest in collaborating with incumbent colleges and universities or by virtue of their intent to displace them.

Notwithstanding the evident diversity of institutions and organizations seeking to tackle matters of employability more directly, it's worth nothing that these schools and companies share many interests: drawing on employer expertise to inform the curriculum design process; exploring the potential to help learners acquire market-relevant skills more rapidly and at lower cost than traditional degrees typically permit; explicitly positioning the cost of their programs relative to the compensation graduates can expect to command in the marketplace; providing students with opportunities to undertake real-world work projects on behalf of prospective employers in the context of their coursework; connecting learners to working professionals who can mentor them as they seek to transition from education to employment; bringing analytics to bear on the assessment of learner success both in academic and professional contexts; drawing on data science to strengthen career services; and treating employers as business partners who possess a shared interest in the success of student-employees and employee-students.

What makes the employability efforts undertaken by these institutions and organizations different from those of most colleges and universities today is their willingness to be explicit about their objectives relative to preparing work-ready graduates, their desire to pilot initiatives that can ultimately operate at scale, and their readiness to step into the world of work while inviting employers to step into the world of higher education in order to conceive and design deeper and more effective ways of collaborating. In those ways, these sorts of efforts point to the potential for an approach to fostering work readiness that could be radically different and more sophisticated than what has come before it. However, as IBM's Jim Spohrer noted, for these sorts of collaborations to become more sophisticated and more common, both universities and industry are going to have to change.

Getting universities and their faculty to welcome industry leaders into the curriculum design process is a major achievement, just as it is for a large corporation to commit to sponsoring and codeveloping a degree program with an education provider or to obligate itself to sending a certain number of employees through a given program. It is a time-consuming and complex process for institutions to incorporate experiential learning opportunities into their courses and degree programs, just as it requires a substantial commitment of time and effort from employers to make internships, co-ops, and apprenticeships more meaningfully connected to the students' areas of academic study. It is all but unprecedented for education providers and employers to collaborate in designing and implementing assessments that capture both the academic and professional components of an education and training experience, and it will challenge educators to define the competencies their curriculum is designed to develop, just as it will challenge employers to conceive of education as preparation for a career rather than preparation for a particular job.

As radical as these concepts may seem, they point to the potential for something even more significant than a more seamless progression from one educational stepping stone to another, as the Obama administration put it. They suggest a different way of conceiving of the roles of education institutions and employers as professional development organizations across the lifetime of the learner: one in which educators go to student-employees where they work in order to combine instruction and experiential learning in a genuinely integrated fashion, and one in which employers step into the classroom or the laboratory or the campus auditorium or the student group meeting in order to more fully develop employee-students' engagement with the curriculum they are studying so that they can more deeply appreciate its relevance to the applied context of work. Such an approach views the transition from education to employment as something more complex than a linear progression; it views it as a cycle in the mode of learn-certify-deploy, learn-certify-deploy, and it requires substantially new behaviors from both universities and their industry partners.

REIMAGINING THE INTEGRATION OF STUDY AND WORK

In aggregate, the diverse models presented here for fostering work readiness among today's undergraduate and graduate students point toward a new vision for the role of colleges or universities in preparing students for the world of work, one that draws on the strengths of contemporary institutional practices but develops them further by reimagining the integration of study and work through a more thoroughgoing collaboration with employers of all types.

According to the results of a recent poll of college and university presidents conducted by Gallup and *Inside Higher Ed,* "nine in 10 presidents said an emphasis on 'critical thinking' skills and personal development is very important throughout college in order for graduates to get jobs," and yet "only about 40 percent of the presidents think their own institutions are very effective" at producing those outcomes.[1] If there is a disconnect here, it isn't because the institutional leaders don't know what would help. In the same survey, a reported 78 percent of presidents responding to the poll said that providing opportunities for students to participate in internships that allow them to apply what they had learned in real-world work settings is "very important," and yet just 38 percent of respondents said that their schools are "good at doing this."

So what will it take for greater numbers of institutions to more effectively prepare their students for the world of work, and what might a vision for a radically reimagined integration of study and work look like? There are a number of actions that stand out as being key components of such a vision.

At the top of the list, perhaps, is leaving aside the technical debates about whether or not a skills gap genuinely exists; educators and employers need to agree on what employability and work readiness look like. The conversation today is, by and large, too fuzzy, as one side promotes the development of qualities such as mindfulness, inquisitiveness, assertiveness, empathy, self-awareness, motivation, curiosity, optimism, and resilience while the other side promotes the development of deep technical skills or relatively narrow knowledge bases in order to speed students' time to that first or next job. Emerging competency-based education models point to some new ways of conceiving of work readiness, but these early efforts at characterizing competency are bound to oscillate between being more academic and institutionally driven and being narrowly technical and job specific and industry driven. Clearly, the set of competencies we would expect an individual to have to master to be judged competent will vary depending on the area of study or the job that needs to be filled. But the definition of work readiness won't be useful if it's wholly different for every possible field of study and every conceivable job.

One of the things that makes degrees attractive as signals of potential in a recruiting context is their convenience; they simplify the hiring process by associating individual graduates with institutional brands. If, as the old saw goes, no one ever got fired for buying IBM, it may be equally true that no recruiter ever got fired for hiring a graduate from a top-ranked school. But recruiting on the basis of competence and work readiness will be more challenging and time consuming, and it will require shared definitions of competence among education providers and employers so that the outcomes achieved by the former align with the expectations and requirements of the latter.

Education providers can help improve the prospects for arriving at a shared understanding of competence if they are also prepared to be in the market and be ready to go where the students are. Consider, for example, how Northeastern University approached its feasibility research on the Charlotte and Seattle markets prior to opening campuses there. In part, the university leadership relied on secondary sources to assess the attractiveness and fit of each market, but it also went into the field and talked with hundreds of employers. When selecting leaders for these new campuses, Northeastern hired individuals who possessed long professional track records in each market and strong reputations among local employers. Alternatively, consider the expansion of internships through NYU's array of study-away sites, which in certain cities was accomplished by working with third parties to assist NYU in forging new relationships with local employers. Or consider how Georgia Tech's veteran transition programs have leveraged the institution's long-standing relationships with the military, particularly in the greater Atlanta area, as well as its relationships with local industry, such as with HP in the information technology sector. These programs are no doubt strengthened by the fact that they are overseen by and delivered by former military personnel. "Being in market" can mean many things, but at its core it requires that university leaders listen to the needs of local employers prior to defining a strategy for serving them and involve them in a substantive way in defining the skills that college graduates must possess in order to be successful in that particular employment market.

To accomplish that, college and university leaders need to think more holistically about how to manage employer partnerships. These relationships can have multiple dimensions—related to internships, recruitment, philanthropy, research collaboration, economic development, vending—and they need to be managed in a way that recognizes the distinct value of each of these dimensions as well as their relation to one another. To do that effectively, institutions need to adopt consistent account management practices with an eye to successfully establishing new partnerships and growing and diversifying existing partnerships. Achieving that will require diverse institutional functions—from corporate relations, to advancement, to career services, to any number of other administrative and academic units—to collaborate in the management and development of these relationships as well as in capturing the insight that can be gleaned from all manner of interactions with these partners to inform the design of curriculum, the shaping of value propositions, the development of go-to-market strategies, and many other decision points.

These concepts are difficult to implement in the real world, of course, particularly when institutions such as a Georgia Tech, NYU, or Northeastern, like so many others, are themselves complex federations of offices, functions, and departments, each serving its own purposes, pursuing its own priorities, and, often times, working with its own distinct record-keeping system. But in order to effectively nurture these partnerships, institutions will have to recognize that they are competing for the attention of employers, and, as a consequence, they must demonstrate the capacity to deliver more value than their competitors—those other institutions that are also seeking to develop relationships with local employers. Optimally, universities need to see themselves as providing strategic business solutions for their employer partners in return for those employers' guidance on programming decisions, enrollment of their employees in those programs, and any number of other supports. That will be more effectively done if institutions can demonstrate the ability to manage diverse aspects of their partnerships in a coordinated way.

Of course, employers have obligations as well. They should seek to understand the opportunities offered by their institutional partners to inform curriculum design, whether by participating in one-on-one interviews, attending curriculum planning meetings, presenting to students in the classroom, or suggesting any additional value-added ways that they would like to become still more involved. Moreover, where appropriate, employers should signal when it may make sense for them to consider investing in the development of more tailored offerings and offer guidance on how many enrollments their organizations might generate for those tailored programs on a going-forward basis. AT&T's partnership with Georgia Tech for the OMS CS represents one model for this kind of investment and enrollment partnership, and the company's partnership with Udacity around nanodegrees represents another variation on the theme, albeit in the context of a relationship with a commercial platform company rather than an accredited, degree-granting institution. The participation of leaders from the Boston area biomedical industry in the design of Northeastern's master's degree in Regulatory Affairs suggests another way of contributing, while the industry colloquia hosted by NYU's Polytechnic School of Engineering is a model of a different kind of value proposition in its creation of intimate opportunities for industry leaders to exchange ideas and network while also providing NYU with insight into their education and training needs.

As the AT&T partnerships with Georgia Tech and Udacity suggest, employers can also inform decisions regarding the particular types of delivery models that best suit them—whether fully online or hybrid or on campus or at the workplace—as well as other forms of customization of curriculum. It will be interesting to see how employer partners come to view the prospective utility of higher education innovations such as the "flipped classroom," where lectures are viewed online so that class time can be devoted to more interactive forms of engagement, as well as adaptive learning tools, with the potential they have for increasingly personalized self-paced learning. Additionally, such partnerships suggest that a willingness on the part of institutions to consider new pricing strategies can stimulate employer interest in collaboration. Indeed, the rapid proliferation of coding academies also underscores the extent to which, in certain disciplines, price-based competition could be key going forward.

Expanding opportunities for experiential learning should be a top priority for institutions and employers because of the many benefits they offer to all stakeholders: universities can use co-ops and other experiential learning activities as opportunities for data gathering to ensure that curricula are up-to-date; employers can benefit by engaging talented students in challenge projects or bringing students on as interns or co-ops in order to evaluate their potential as permanent hires; and students have the opportunity to demonstrate their skills in real-world settings, learn how to put the tools of the workplace to use, and discover where their deep interests align with longer-term employment opportunities. Apart from challenge projects, internships, and co-ops, there are other powerful ways that experiential learning opportunities can be structured. Consider Northeastern's pilot course in project management, NYU's Business Boot Camp for the Liberal Arts, the mini-mester noncredit courses currently being envisaged at Georgia

Tech—learning opportunities such as these can assist students in developing portfolios of work product that can assist them as they seek to promote their talents and capabilities on entering the job market.

Ultimately, deeper collaboration around the definition of work readiness, curriculum design, delivery models, and experiential learning opportunities opens up the opportunity for institution and employer collaboration around assessment. Competency-based education models present one such opportunity, but there is room for other approaches. Certainly students would benefit from an assessment model that evaluated their academic accomplishments in ways that were not so dissimilar to how their professional contributions are likely to be measured. Currently, there is no lingua franca that can function effectively in both contexts. For the most part, performance of students in the classroom is scored with letter grades, while the performance of employees is typically assessed in terms of high, medium, or low performance in areas such as reaching business targets, contributing effectively to teams, customer or partnership management, and so on. Recently, the testing company ACT began offering a National Career Readiness Certificate that "measures 'soft skills' like work discipline, teamwork, customer service skills, and managerial potential."[2] Other assessment firms and testing companies are developing inventories of their own. The opportunity here is enormous, but that task is complex. Yet, as institutions and employers become more intimately involved in one another's worlds, greater collaboration around assessment must be a natural result.

If partnerships of this sort can be formed, developed, and deepened, and if universities can demonstrate the capacity to manage a growing number of such partnerships in a more holistic and coordinated fashion, then a broader opportunity opens up to treat these relationships as part of a larger network, or ecosystem, that connects faculty, staff, students, alumni, industry recruiters, and other stakeholders as members of a single community that generates multiple forms of value for all participants. This is no doubt how Northeastern imagines its thousands of employer partnerships will function through the continued development of its Global Network, and certainly this kind of ecosystem is similar in many respects to the type of community network NYU aims to establish with its NY You platform.

It is a curious fact of higher education that for most of their histories our institutions of higher learning have largely dissuaded their graduates from returning to acquire additional credentials, presumably because this was thought to narrow students' educational experiences unnecessarily. Today, one would be hard-pressed to find a college or university that isn't interested in providing some kind of further educational benefit to its alumni. In a future scenario such as the one imagined by the writers of Georgia Tech's strategic plan, where students enroll for shorter stretches of time more frequently over the course of their careers and lifetimes, it makes sense for institutions to think about customer retention, and community-based ecosystems such as the one envisioned by NYU have the potential to play a key role for alumni as the dominant educational paradigm continues its evolution from a linear education-to-employment model to a cyclical learn-certify-deploy, learn-certify-deploy model, or even some other model characterized by a more integrated blending of study and work. Building lifelong relationships with a community of learners in this fashion has the potential not only to connect prospective students with current students or current students with alumni who can serve as mentors but also to foster deeper relationships with the employers of alumni, which can, in turn, drive philanthropy, research collaboration, enrollment growth, long-term brand loyalty, and reputation enhancement, among other benefits.

CRANKSHAFT'S LEGACY

Gradually, the notion of the Ivory Tower is being supplanted by the prototype of a networked university, where the unique character of its relationships with its employer partners becomes the source of the institution's value proposition and competitive advantage. Whether we call it Drownproofing 2.0, Liberal Education 2.0, or something else, there appears to be increasingly widespread agreement within the higher education community that a focus on employability today is critical. Fred Lanoue initiated a form of survival training at Georgia Tech that has evolved into an institutional ethos about resolve, persistence, readiness, and the entrepreneurial spirit. Almost seventy-five years after the launch of his course in water-survival skills, that ethos is now spreading from institution to institution.

What universities like Georgia Tech, NYU, Northeastern, and many of the other institutions examined here show is that the turn to employability can build on long-standing organizational strengths while providing opportunities to innovate in ways that make the paradigm for higher education more closely attuned to the needs of the current economic climate. As a consequence, the risk facing many colleges and universities today is less of embracing the Drownproofing 2.0 imperative than it is of taking no action. Institutions left standing on the sidelines will not only face more intense competition for students from the college and university peers, but they will also risk being supplanted by an array of entrepreneurial ventures seeking to connect students with marketable skills and career opportunities.

For some institutions, embracing employability as an objective for their students will require a new philosophical disposition about the purpose of higher education and an evolved value system with respect to the relationship between education and training. It will mean conceiving of their audiences differently—not just students and parents but employers and employees, professional associations, government agencies, and more—as well as conceiving of how best to effectively reach and serve those audiences, whether locally or around the world, on campus or online, or some combination of the two. It will also mean thinking in new ways about their own institutional core competencies and where and how to effectively outsource or partner with third parties to bring certain benefits to their students, third parties such as commercial solution providers or other institutions that possess complementary core competencies.

For virtually all institutions, tackling the challenges and opportunities associated with supporting employability will require a continuous evolution of institutional roles and organizational structures as well as leadership recruitment strategies in order to effectively support more extensive, better-coordinated, and increasingly professionalized activity in the realms of online learning, content modularization, experiential learning, social networking platforms, partnership management, and competitive positioning, among other areas. As institutional partnerships with employers become more complex and numerous, it will also be incumbent on each college or university to devise strategies for managing these relationships: whether they should each be treated as a one-to-one partnership, whether the institution should position itself in a one-to-many relation with a diverse portfolio of partnerships, whether the institution should elect to forge a community supporting many-to-many collaborations for the diversity of stakeholders within its own branded ecosystem, or some combination of these.

Higher education is changing in many ways—from how it is funded, to how it is regulated, to how its institutions are governed, to how they conceive of their value propositions and cost structures and business models, to how students and parents view education-related debt and the return on their educational investment, and more. Indeed, in the 2035 envisioned by Georgia Tech in the process of developing its strategic plan, the world of higher education looks different. Between now and then, college and university leaders will have to ask themselves what being different will mean for each institution.

At the start of the recession in 2008, people within the higher education community were guessing about when things would return to normal; then the discussion turned to something called "the new normal." Things are different since the recession. One big difference is the global focus on economic development and job creation, which has stimulated a broad discussion about a purported skills gap, underemployment and unemployment, unfilled job openings, and the need to better orient our colleges and universities to the task of preparing work-ready graduates who can thrive amid these new economic realities—not least, perhaps, by striking the entrepreneurial spark themselves and creating their own jobs.

The cases examined here should provoke further reflection—among university leaders, employers, policy makers—about how our institutions of higher education can harness their strengths in new and different ways to tackle these challenges and opportunities supported by their employer partners and other participants in their local ecosystems. Drownproofing 1.0, as Lanoue designed it, could be accomplished on a college campus, relying only on the guidance of a qualified instructor. But developing the kind of life skills required by the Drownproofing 2.0 imperative will demand new and deeper levels of collaboration among the diverse participants in today's talent development ecosystem and, ultimately, a more thoughtful and thoroughgoing integration of study and work.

NOTES

FOREWORD

1. Bengt-Aake Lundvall, "Understanding the Role of Education in the Learning Economy: The Contribution of Economics," in *Knowledge Management in the Learning Society* (Paris: OECD, 2000).
2. Claudia Goldin and L. F. Katz, *The Race Between Education and Technology* (Cambridge, MA: Harvard University Press, 2008).
3. Ibid., 12.
4. Susan J. Schurman and Louis Soares, "Connecting the Dots: Creating a Postsecondary Education System for the 21st-Century Workforce," in *Transforming the U.S. Workforce Development System: Lessons from Research and Practice* (Champaign, IL: Labor and Employment Relations Association, University of Illinois at Urbana-Champaign, 2010).
5. D. Lepak and S. Snell, "Managing the Human Resource Architecture for Knowledge-Based Competition," in *Managing Knowledge for Sustained Competitive Advantage: Designing Strategies for Effective Human Resource Management*, ed. S. Jackson, M. Hitt, and A. DeNisi (San Francisco: Jossey-Bass, 2003), 127–154.
6. Michael E. Porter, "Workforce Development in the Global Economy" (presentation, Inter-American Development Bank, Washington, DC, November 18, 2002).
7. Clayton M. Christensen and Michael E. Raynor, *The Innovator's Solution: Creating and Sustaining Successful Growth* (Cambridge, MA: Harvard Business Press, 2003).

INTRODUCTION

1. Melissa Korn, "Are Colleges Producing Career-Ready Graduates?" *Wall Street Journal*, September 3, 2014.

2. Dan Berrett, "Do Americans Expect Too Much from a College Degree?" *Chronicle of Higher Education*, September 2, 2014.

3. Robert Reich, "College Is a Ludicrous Waste of Money," *Salon*, September 3, 2014.

4. See the BioNetwork, Project Quest, http://www.ncbionetwork.org; http://www.questsa.org/index.html; and the Automotive Manufacturing Technical Education Collaborative at the Kentucky Community and Technical College System, http://www.kctcs.edu/en/System _Initiatives/AMTEC.aspx.

5. National Center for Education Statistics, IPEDS Data Center, http:// nces.ed.gov/ipeds/datacenter/.

CHAPTER 1

1. See Georgia Tech Alumni Association, http://gtalumni.org/Publications /techtopics/fall94/escape.html; http://en.wikipedia.org/wiki /Drownproofing; http://en.wikipedia.org/wiki/Georgia_Tech _traditions#Drownproofing; and http://buzzpedia.lmc.gatech.edu /wiki/index.php/Drownproofing.

2. Steve McLaughlin, Steve W. Chaddick School Chair of the School of Electrical and Computer Engineering, Georgia Institute of Technology, in discussion with the author, January 22, 2014.

3. Beckie Supiano, "So Your College Offers Students an 'Employment Guarantee'?" *Chronicle of Higher Education*, September 18, 2014.

4. Scott Jaschik, "Obama's Ratings for Higher Ed," *Inside Higher Ed*, August 22, 2013.

5. Barack Obama, interview by David Karp, June 10, 2014, http://www .officialwire.com/pr/remarks-by-the-president-in-qa-with-david-karp -ceo-of-tumblr/.

6. "Ready to Work: New Actions to Expand Job-Driven Training and Broaden the Pathway to the Middle Class" (press release, the White House, July 22, 2014), http://www.whitehouse.gov/sites/default/files /ready_to_work_factsheet_finalembargoed_7_21_14.pdf.

7. Robert Lerman, "Expanding Apprenticeship Opportunities in the United States" (report, the Hamilton Project, June 2014).

8. Cliff Peale, "Employers Go to College to Guide Worker Training," *Cincinnati Enquirer*, June 8, 2014.

9. Melissa Korn, "Colleges Are Tested by Push to Prove Graduates' Career Success," *Wall Street Journal*, March 17, 2014.

10. Katy Barnato, "MIT Triumphs in New World University Rankings," CNBC, September 16, 2014, http://www.cnbc.com/id/102003187.

11. Michael Porter, "The New Role of Business in Global Education: How Companies Can Create Shared Value by Improving Education While Driving Shareholder Returns" (report, FSG, January 15, 2014).

12. Douglas Belkin and Caroline Porter, "Corporate Cash Alters University Curricula," *Wall Street Journal*, April 7, 2014.

13. "Chancellor Zimpher Sets Forth Bold Plan to Expand Access to SUNY's Top Quality, Affordable Education in 2014 State of the University Address" (press release, State University of New York, January 14, 2014).

14. John Fry, "Put Undergraduates to Work, for Their Own Good," *Chronicle of Higher Education*, January 20, 2014.

15. Ibid.

16. Dan Berrett, "Clark U. Seeks to Define 'Liberal Education 2.0,'" *Chronicle of Higher Education*, June 23, 2014.

17. Rebecca Strong, "Liberal Arts Schools Address Skills Gap with Experiential Learning," *U.S. News & World Report*, July 20, 2014.

18. Wendy Purcell, "Employability Is Our Job," *Inside Higher Ed*, June 13, 2014.

19. Mona Mourshed, Jigar Patel, and Katrin Suder, "Education to Employment: Getting Europe's Youth into Works" (report, McKinsey & Co., January 2014).

20. Ibid.

21. Mona Mourshed, Diana Farrell, and Dominic Barton, "Education to Employment: Designing a System That Works" (report, McKinsey & Co., December, 2012).

22. Purcell, "Employability Is Our Job."

23. Kenneth Freeman, "The World Has Changed Since the Industrial Revolution, but Universities Have Not," *Wall Street Journal*, October 14, 2013.

24. Lee Newman, "Corporate Recruiters: Stop Your Short-Term Thinking," ibid., October 14, 2013.

25. Fry, "Put Undergraduates to Work, for Their Own Good."

26. Peter Cappelli, "If There's a Gap, Blame It on the Employer," *New York Times*, August 3, 2012.

27. Walter Frick, "The Hardest Roles to Hire For," *Harvard Business Review*, July 2, 2014.

28. Ibid.

29. Jonathan Rothwell, "Still Searching: Job Vacancies and STEM Skills" (report, Brookings Institution, July 2014), 15.

30. James Bessen, "Employers Aren't Just Whining—the 'Skills Gap' Is Real," *Harvard Business Review*, August 25, 2014.

31. Lauren Weber, "Apprenticeships Help Close the Skills Gap. So Why Are They in Decline?" *Wall Street Journal*, April 27, 2014.

32. "Ready to Work."

33. Carl Straumsheim, "Shrinking Cal State Online," *Inside Higher Ed*, July 22, 2014.

34. Carl Straumsheim, "Identifying the Online Student," ibid., June 3, 2014.

35. See Scott Jaschik, "Harvard Profs Push Back," ibid., May 28, 2013; Ry Rivard, "Duke Faculty Say No," ibid., April 30, 2013; "Rutgers Graduate Faculty Rejects Online Degree Compromise," ibid., May 9, 2014; and Carl Straumsheim, "Rifts in the Valley," ibid., November 19, 2013.

36. Mourshed, Farrell, and Barton, "Education to Employment."

37. Michael Porter, "Clusters and the New Economics of Competition," *Harvard Business Review* (November–December 1998): 77–90.

38. Thomas Kochan, David Finefold, and Paul Osterman, "Who Can Fix the 'Middle-Skills' Gap?" 90 (December 2012): 81–90.

39. It is important to distinguish between *certificates,* which many accredited colleges and universities offer, and *certifications,* which are typically a form of recognition bestowed on a learner who has completed one or another type of practical training by a professional association or other unaccredited organization, such as a software company. Certifications have value in the employer marketplace, but they are not degrees or credentials in the same sense as an undergraduate degree or master's certificate.

40. Eduardo Porter, "A Smart Way to Skip College in Pursuit of a Job," *New York Times*, June 17, 2014.

41. Ibid.

42. Ibid.

43. Douglas Belkin and Caroline Porter, "Corporate Cash Alters University Curricula," *Wall Street Journal*, April 7, 2014.

44. Melissa Korn, "The End of College As We Know It (and Students Feel Fine)," *Wall Street Journal*, June 8, 2014.

45. Steve Kolowich, "Would Graduate School Work Better If You Never Graduated from It?" *Chronicle of Higher Education*, July 17, 2014.

CHAPTER 2

1. Megan Rogers, "Rensselaer Polytechnic Institute to Offer IBM-Designed Classes," *Albany Business Review,* May 8, 2014.
2. Marc Parry, "Competency-Based Education Advances with U.S. Approval of Program," *Chronicle of Higher Education,* April 18, 2013.
3. See College for America, http://collegeforamerica.org.
4. Paul Fain, "Experimental College's First Graduate," *Inside Higher Ed,* August 16, 2013.
5. Paul Fain, "Taking the Direct Path," ibid., February 21, 2014.
6. Paul Fain, "Experimenting with Aid," ibid., July 23, 2014.
7. Ibid.
8. "Chancellor Zimpher Sets Forth Bold Plan to Expand Access to SUNY's Top Quality, Affordable Education in 2014 State of the University Address" (press release, the State University of New York, January 14, 2014), http://www.suny.edu/suny-news/press-releases/january-2014/1-14-14chancellor-zimpher-sets-forth-bold-plan-to-/.
9. Kaitlin Gambrill, assistant vice chancellor for Strategic Planning and University Advancement, the State University of New York, in discussion with the author, January 28, 2014.
10. See Dartmouth College, http://www.tuck.dartmouth.edu/undergradbiz/.
11. Laura Colarusso, "Students Paying Extra for Business Skills They Say They Haven't Learned on Campus," *Hechinger Report,* July 8, 2014.
12. Ishani Premaratne, "Bridge Programs Aim to Fill Liberal Arts Gap," *USA Today,* April 1, 2013.
13. Ibid.
14. Allie Grasgreen, "New Job for Career Services," *Inside Higher Ed,* January 21, 2014.
15. Ibid.
16. Bob Karp, senior Industrial Liaison officer, Massachusetts Institute of Technology, in discussion with the author, June 19, 2014.
17. Karp, June 19, 2014.
18. "Harvard Business School Launches HBX," *Harvard Magazine,* March 21, 2014.
19. The HBX Web site warns that prices could rise in the future. See http://hbx.hbs.edu/hbx-core/core-faqs.html#core-cost.
20. Jerry Useem, "Business School, Disrupted," *New York Times,* May 31, 2014.
21. See CB Insights, http://www.cbinsights.com/blog/ed-tech-deals-bubble.

22. John Cook, "Onvia Co-Founder Raises $4.35M for Koru, Helping College Grads Find Impactful Jobs," *GeekWire*, December 12, 2013.

23. Ingrid Lunden, "General Assembly Raises $35M Led by New Investor IVP to Add More Tech Courses, New Campuses," *TechCrunch,* March 7, 2014.

24. Sarah Mitroff, "The Minerva Project Raises Largest-Ever Seed Funding from Benchmark for Elite University," *Venture Beat,* April 3, 2012.

25. See the Fullbridge Program, https://fullbridge.com/our-story/.

26. *The Fullbridge Program* (brochure, Fullbridge, 2014).

27. Paul Fain, "XBA Certificate for Veterans," *Inside Higher Ed*, August 8, 2014.

28. See Startup Institute, http://www.startupinstitute.com.

29. Colarusso, "Students Paying Extra."

30. Josh Jarrett, chief learning officer, Koru, in discussion with the author, March 7, 2014.

31. See Koru, http://www.joinkoru.com/college_partner.

32. *The Fullbridge Program*.

33. See Dream Careers, http://www.summerinternships.com/about-us/.

34. See Dream Careers, http://www.summerinternships.com/educators/.

35. See Black Mountain SOLE, http://blackmountainsole.org/about/.

36. "Black Mountain SOLE Raises $5M for DIY School," *EdSurge,* May 12, 2013.

37. See Collegefeed, https://www.collegefeed.com.

38. Brandon Bailey, "Q&A: Sanjeev Agrawal, CEO of Collegefeed, on Finding Jobs for Grads," *Mercury News,* May 9, 2014.

39. See Collegefeed, https://www.collegefeed.com.

40. See AfterCollege, http://www.aftercollege.com/content/about_aftercollege.

41. See Evisors, http://www.evisors.com.

42. See ModernGuild, http://modernguild.com//sites/all/modules/guild/mg/jquery-datatable/mg-homepage_ecommerce-v2/index.php#.

43. See Doostang, http://www.doostang.com.

44. See Accredible, https://www.accredible.com.

45. See Credly, https://credly.com.

46. Iris Mansour, "Degreed Wants to Make Online Courses Count," *Fortune,* August 15, 2013.

47. Ibid.

48. Ibid.

49. See Mindsumo, https://www.mindsumo.com/home.

50. See Coursolve, https://www.coursolve.org.

51. See RadMatter, http://radmatter.com.

52. See WorkAmerica, http://www.workamerica.co/jobseeker.html.

53. Paul Fain, "Have Job, Will Enroll," *Inside Higher Ed*, May 23, 2014.

54. See Workforce.IO, http://www.workforce.io.

55. See Career Sushi, http://www.careersushi.com.

56. See Gild, http://www.gild.com.

57. See Pymetrics, https://pymetrics.com.

58. See Kalibrr, https://www.kalibrr.com.

59. Elizabeth Sile, "The Future of Venture for America," *Inc.*, August 15, 2011.

60. See Venture for America, http://ventureforamerica.org.

61. Ingrid Lunden, "LinkedIn Growing up: Opens up to High School Students over 13, Launches Dedicated Pages for Universities Worldwide," *TechCrunch*, August 19, 2013.

62. Lauren Hepler, "LinkedIn Moves to Legitimize Web Classes by Coursera, Udacity, Others," *Silicon Valley Business Journal*, November 14, 2013.

63. Charlie Tyson, "The New Rankings?" *Inside Higher Ed*, August 14, 2014.

64. See General Assembly, https://generalassemb.ly.

65. See Hack Reactor, http://www.hackreactor.com.

66. Shawn Drost, lead instructor and chief commercial officer, Hack Reactor, in discussion with the author, October 16, 2013.

67. See Launch Academy, http://www.launchacademy.com.

68. See Marker Square, http://www.makersquare.com.

69. See Dev Bootcamp, http://devbootcamp.com.

70. "Kaplan Acquires Dev Bootcamp, Founder and Leader of the Software Developer Bootcamp Industry" (press release, Kaplan, June 25, 2014), http://www.businesswire.com/news/home/20140625005645/en/Kaplan-Acquires-Dev-Bootcamp-Founder-Leader-Software#.VKGKJAwmk.

71. See Flat Iron School, http://flatironschool.com.

72. See Lynda.com, http://www.lynda.com.

73. See Code Avengers, http://www.codeavengers.com.

74. J. J. Colao, "Codecademy Raises $10 Million to Conquer the World," *Forbes*, June 19, 2012.

75. See Codeacademy, http://www.codecademy.com.

76. Mary Beth Marklein, "A Cheaper, Faster Version of a College Degree," *USA Today*, July 11, 2014.

77. Clarissa Shen, "Announcing Nanodegrees: A New Type of Credential for a Modern Workforce," Udacity blog, June 16, 2014.

78. Ibid.

79. Tim Walker, "Will the Minerva Project—the First 'Elite' American University to Be Launched in a Century—Change the Face of Higher Learning?" *The Independent,* July 24, 2014.

80. Ibid.

81. Doug Lederman, "Minerva Plans Annual Price of $29,000 for Online Residential Program," *Inside Higher Ed,* September 18, 2013.

82. Walker, "Will the Minerva Project . . ."

83. Scott Jaschik, "Minerva Finds Partner for Accreditation," *Inside Higher Ed,* July 24, 2013.

CHAPTER 3

1. See Georgia Institute of Technology, President's Office, http://www.president.gatech.edu/about-dr-peterson.

2. "Designing the Future: A Strategic Vision and Plan" (strategic plan, Georgia Institute of Technology, August, 2010), 8.

3. Steve McLaughlin, Steve W. Chaddick School Chair, School of Electrical and Computer Engineering, Georgia Institute of Technology, in discussion with the author, January 22, 2014.

4. Nelson Baker, dean of Professional Education, Georgia Institute of Technology, in discussion with the author, April 30, 2014.

5. Baker, April 30, 2014.

6. "Deal: With Deep Freeze over, Georgia's Economy Warms" (press release, Office of the Governor, January 14, 2014), http://gov.georgia.gov/press-releases/2014-01-15/deal-deep-freeze-over-georgia's-economy-warms.

7. Leo Mark, associate dean for Academic Programs and Student Affairs, Professional Education, Georgia Institute of Technology, in discussion with the author, January 17, 2014.

8. Steve Kolowich, "Would Graduate School Work Better If You Never Graduated from It?" *Chronicle of Higher Education,* July 17, 2014.

9. "Designing the Future," 16.

10. Ibid., 11.

11. Ibid., 4.

12. Ibid., 5.

13. Ibid.

14. Ibid., 3.

15. Doug Williams, senior associate chair of the School of Electrical and Computer Engineering, Georgia Institute of Technology, in discussion with the author, April 30, 2014.

16. Williams, April 30, 2014.

17. Greg King, strategic partners officer, Enterprise Innovation Institute, Georgia Institute of Technology, in discussion with the author, May 1, 2014.

18. Zvi Galil, dean of the College of Computing, Georgia Institute of Technology, in discussion with the author, January 27, 2014.

19. Williams, April 30, 2014.

20. Williams, April 30, 2014.

21. Charles Isbell, senior associate dean of the College of Computing, Georgia Institute of Technology, in discussion with the author, February 4, 2014.

22. King, January 24, 2014.

23. King, January 24, 2014.

24. Galil, January 27, 2014.

25. Baker, April 30, 2014.

26. Baker, April 30, 2014.

27. McLaughlin, January 22, 2014.

28. Williams, April 30, 2014.

29. Isbell, May 1, 2014.

30. See Georgia Tech Capstone Design Expo, http://www.capstone.gatech .edu.

31. Isbell, February 4, 2014.

32. Isbell, May 1, 2014.

33. Williams, January 24, 2014.

34. Williams, April 30, 2014.

35. McLaughlin, January 22, 2014.

36. See Georgia Tech Professional Education, http://gtpe.gatech.edu /military-transition-program.

37. Mark, January 17, 2014.

38. See Georgia Tech Professional Education, http://gtpe.gatech.edu /military-transition-program.

39. "HP Partners with WOS to Train Veterans for Critical Roles" (press release, Workforce Opportunity Services, undated), http://www.wforce .org/index.php/news/212-hp-partners-with-wos-to-train-veterans-for -critical-roles.

40. "Helping Veterans Transition to the Workforce," *The Buzz at Student Affairs* (newsletter, Georgia Institute of Technology, September 23, 2013), http://parentnews.gatech.edu/hg/item/239731.
41. Mark, January 17, 2014.
42. Ry Rivard, "Massive (but Not Open)," *Inside Higher Ed*, May 14, 2013.
43. Ibid.
44. Baker, April 30, 2014.
45. Baker, April 30, 2014.
46. Baker, April 30, 2014.
47. Baker, August 8, 2014.
48. Baker, April 30, 2014.
49. Baker, April 30, 2014.
50. Carl Straumsheim, "The First Cohort," *Inside Higher Ed*, December 13, 2013.
51. Isbell, May 1, 2014.
52. Baker, April 30, 2014.
53. Isbell, May 1, 2014.
54. Baker, April 30, 2014.
55. Isbell, May 1, 2014.
56. Isbell, May 1, 2014.
57. King, January 24, 2014.
58. Isbell, February 4, 2014.
59. Mark, January 17 and May 1, 2014.
60. Isbell, May 1, 2014.
61. Baker, April 30, 2014.

CHAPTER 4

1. See National Science Foundation, https://ncsesdata.nsf.gov/profiles/site;jsessionid=F074FCA3FF5B6E420DCE7FB2254C71AB?method=rankingBySource&ds=herd.
2. John Sexton, "Global Network University Reflection," December 21, 2010, http://www.nyu.edu/about/leadership-university-administration/office-of-the-president/redirect/speeches-statements/global-network-university-reflection.html.
3. See Institute of International Education, http://www.iie.org/Research-and-Publications/Open-Doors/Data/International-Students/Leading-Institutions/2012-13.
4. See http://en.wikipedia.org/wiki/New_York_University_Polytechnic_School_of_Engineering.

5. John Sexton, "NYU Abu Dhabi and Our Global Future," fall 2007, http://www.nyu.edu/about/leadership-university-administration /office-of-the-president/redirect/speeches-statements/nyu-abu-dhabi -and-our-global-future.html.

6. Linda Mills, vice chancellor for Global Programs and University Life, New York University, and associate vice chancellor for Admissions and Financial Support, NYU Abu Dhabi, in discussion with the author, January 8, 2014.

7. Mills, January 8, 2014.

8. Dennis Di Lorenzo, dean of the School of Professional Studies, New York University, in discussion with the author, January 9, 2014.

9. Rachel Aviv, "The Imperial Presidency," *The New Yorker*, September 9, 2013.

10. Sexton, "Global Network University Reflection."

11. Ibid.

12. Ibid.

13. Jim Sleeper, "Liberal Education in Authoritarian Places," *New York Times*, August 31, 2013.

14. Sexton, "Global Network University Reflection."

15. Ibid.

16. Sleeper, "Liberal Education in Authoritarian Places."

17. Sexton, "Global Network University Reflection."

18. Trudy Steinfeld, assistant vice president for Student Affairs and executive director of the Wasserman Center for Career Development, New York University, in discussion with the author, January 7, 2014.

19. Steinfeld, January 7, 2014.

20. Matthew Santirocco, senior vice provost for Undergraduate Academic Affairs, New York University, in discussion with the author, January 10, 2014.

21. Santirocco, January 10, 2014.

22. Mills, January 8, 2014.

23. Santirocco, January 10, 2014.

24. Santirocco, January 10, 2014.

25. Santirocco, January 10, 2014.

26. Santirocco, January 10, 2014.

27. Di Lorenzo, March 13, 2014.

28. Di Lorenzo, January 9, 2014.

29. Di Lorenzo, January 9, 2014.

30. Steinfeld, January 7, 2014.

31. Steinfeld, January 7, 2014.

32. Santirocco, March 12, 2014.

33. Bob Ubell, vice dean of Online Learning, NYU Polytechnic School of Engineering, New York University, in discussion with the author, January 10, 2014.

34. Ubell, January 10, 2014.

35. Ubell, March 12, 2014.

36. Ubell, January 10, 2014.

37. Ubell, March 12, 2014.

38. Ubell, January 10, 2014.

39. Ubell, January 10, 2014.

40. Ubell, January 10, 2014.

41. Ubell, March 12, 2014.

42. Thomas Kochan, David Finefold, and Paul Osterman, "Who Can Fix the 'Middle-Skills' Gap?" 90 (December 2012): 81–90.

43. Eitan Zemel, dean of Business and Engineering, NYU Shanghai, and vice dean of Global Programs and Executive Programs, Leonard N. Stern School of Business, New York University, in discussion with the author, January 9, 2014.

44. Zemel, January 9, 2014.

45. Erin O'Brien, associate dean of Global Programs and Executive Programs, Leonard N. Stern School of Business, New York University, in discussion with the author, January 9, 2014.

46. Zemel, January 9, 2014.

47. O'Brien, January 9, 2014.

48. Di Lorenzo, January 9, 2014.

49. Di Lorenzo, January 9, 2014.

50. Di Lorenzo, January 9, 2014.

51. Di Lorenzo, March 13, 2014.

52. Di Lorenzo, March 13, 2014.

53. Steinfeld, January 7, 2014.

54. Richard Matasar, vice president for University Enterprise Initiatives, New York University, in discussion with the author, March 13, 2014.

55. Matasar, March 13, 2014.

56. Matasar, March 13, 2014.

57. Matasar, March 13, 2014.

58. Matasar, March 13, 2014.

CHAPTER 5

1. See Northeastern University, http://www.northeastern.edu /accomplishments/#innovation and http://en.wikipedia.org/wiki /Northeastern_University.
2. See Northeastern University, http://www.northeastern.edu /accomplishments/#innovation.
3. See Institute of International Education, http://www.iie.org/Research -and-Publications/Open-Doors/Data/International-Students/Leading -Institutions/2012-13.
4. Joseph E. Aoun, president, Northeastern University, in discussion with the author, June 30, 2014. All statements by Aoun in the chapter are from this interview.
5. Sean Gallagher, chief strategy officer, Northeastern University, in discussion with the author, June 10, 2014. All statements by Gallagher in the chapter are from this interview.
6. John LaBrie, dean of the College of Professional Studies and vice president for Professional Education, Northeastern University, in discussion with the author, June 10, 2014. All statements by LaBrie in the chapter are from this interview.
7. Ellen Stoddard, director of Cooperative Education, College of Professional Studies, Northeastern University, in discussion with the author, February 12, 2014. All statements by Stoddard in the chapter are from this interview.
8. Tevis Spezia, "The Learning by Giving Foundation and Northeastern University Award $150,000 in Grants through Giving with Purpose MOOC on Effective Charitable Giving" (press release, Learning by Giving Foundation, June 9, 2014), http://finance.yahoo.com/news /learning-giving-foundation-northeastern-university-191700309 .html.
9. See Northeastern University, http://www.northeastern.edu/align /about-align-program/.

CHAPTER 6

1. Ry Rivard, "Job Skills Expectations Unmet," *Inside Higher Ed*, August 28, 2014.
2. Michael McShane, "Tracking the 'Career' in College and Career Ready," *AEI Ideas*, August 27, 2014, https://www.aei.org/publication /tracking-the-career-in-college-and-career-ready/.

ACKNOWLEDGMENTS

A book such as this is the result of many conversations, some lasting years. Numerous individuals have contributed to the evolving dialogue that spurred the development of this book, though I am the only one who can be blamed for its contents. I'm grateful for the guidance, insight, and inspiration that my friends, colleagues, and family members have provided along the way.

In particular, I thank Joseph Aoun, who, in addition to offering me the opportunity to witness up close how a rising research university such as Northeastern has continued to innovate around the integration of study and work, provided me with the most precious resource needed to bring a project such as this to completion—time.

I owe special thanks to both Nelson Baker at the Georgia Institute of Technology and Rick Matasar at New York University for taking an interest in my project and for introducing me to so many of their colleagues who are out there day after day building better universities. Without Nelson and Rick's early assistance, encouragement, and collaboration, I would have had an idea but not a book. I owe an enormous thanks to their many colleagues, including Zvi Galil, Charles Isbell, Greg King,

Leo Mark, Steve McLaughlin, and Doug Williams at Georgia Tech and Dennis DiLorenzo, Erin O'Brien, Linda Mills, Matthew Santirocco, Trudy Steinfeld, Bob Ubell, and Eitan Zemel at NYU, who made themselves available for multiple interviews and gave generously of their time and their thinking.

I also owe a great debt of appreciation to my former Northeastern University colleagues Sean Gallagher, John LaBrie, and Ellen Stoddard, who showed me both what it takes to conceive of an institution dedicated to experiential learning and what it takes to make it real. I am also grateful for the contributions of my industry colleagues Shawn Drost, Kaitlin Gambrill, Josh Jarrett, and Bob Karp; they added significantly to my understanding of the opportunities related to employability at key moments in the development of this effort.

I thank Doug Lederman, who allowed me to test drive some of the ideas developed here in commentaries at *Inside Higher Ed*. Special thanks to Laura Madden for inquiring about my interest in undertaking a project such as this. And many thanks to my friend Thor Clausen for his endless encouragement and support as I made my way through this effort week by week.

And, most of all, I wish to thank my wife, Lori Stokes, for making everything I endeavor to do possible and for making every day worthwhile.

ABOUT THE AUTHOR

Over the course of a twenty-year career in higher education, Peter Stokes has been employed as a teacher, researcher, consultant, business leader, writer, and university administrator. Today he works as a managing director in the higher education practice at Huron Consulting Group. He lives just outside of Boston with his wife and two children.

INDEX